"The more I read, the more I was touched and, interestingly, found myself saying, 'I WISH I HAD HAD THIS BOOK MANY YEARS AGO.' I kept wishing I had been the kind of husband she describes. THIS BOOK IS RIGHT ON TARGET, especially in a sophisticated, secular, relativistic culture."

—Richard Halverson
Former Chaplain, United States Senate

"*Liberated Through Submission* is DELIGHTFUL TO READ! Just as Bunny has you laughing and enjoying yourself, a powerful truth walks in the back door to surprise you. Her own struggles make the biblical exhortations RELATABLE, TANGIBLE AND PRACTICAL. Your faith will be greatly increased and submission will become A POSITIVE CONCEPT in a day when it is so questioned."

—Vonette Bright
Campus Crusade for Christ

"In a day when the concept of submission is not only misunderstood but often categorically rejected, Bunny Wilson has emerged to provide us A COMPREHENSIVE, PERSONALIZED AND WELL-ILLUSTRATED EXPLANATION of what submission really means from God's perspective. Her CLARITY, INSIGHT AND RELEVANCY will provide every reader, whether husband, wife or single person, with the tools necessary for building or rebuilding their life or family in a positive way in accordance with God's design."

—Dr. Tony Evans
Pastor, Oakcliff Bible Fellowship
Dallas, Texas

"This is probably the MOST EXCELLENT BOOK dealing with not only the wife's role, but also the responsibility of a husband, father, businessman, churchman, single person and everybody else regarding this whole idea of submitting to one another. This book describes how submission works, the dynamics of it and how it could, if practiced, bring joy and happiness to our world. This is A BOOK TO BUY, READ AND PRACTICE.

—Dr. E.V. Hill
Mt. Zion Missionary Baptist Church
Los Angeles, California

LIBERATED
Through
SUBMISSION

P. B. Wilson

HARVEST HOUSE PUBLISHERS

EUGENE, OREGON

LIBERATED THROUGH SUBMISSION
Copyright © 1990 by P.B. Wilson
Published by Harvest House Publishers
Eugene, Oregon 97402
www.harvesthousepublishers.com

Library of Congress Cataloging-in-Publication Data
    Wilson, P.B., 1950-
    Liberated through submission: God's design for freedom in all relationships
    / P.B. Wilson.
    ISBN-13: 978-0-7369-1887-9
    ISBN-10: 0-7369-1887-6
    1. Obedience—Religious aspects—Christianity. 2. Meekness. 3. Evil,
    Nonresistance to. I. Title.
    BV4647.02W54 1990   90-36386
    234'.6—dc20   CIP

Printed in the United States of America

06 07 08 09 10 11 12 13 / VP-MS / 10 9 8 7 6 5 4 3 2 1

To a man who has spent all of our married life "looking beyond my faults and seeing my needs." You are a rare man indeed to have waited (and, in some cases, are still waiting) for God to mold and shape me. This book is dedicated to my companion, leader and best friend, Frank Wilson.

Acknowledgments

I would like to thank Les Stobbe, Matt Parker, Margie Hill, Marilyn Davis and the Wednesday Morning Women's Fellowship. You encouraged me to believe that I could write this book.

To two dear friends, Renee Walker and Mattie Bell, who worked with me to the end—I appreciate you.

To my children: Tracey, Launi, Fawn and Christy Joy. I adore and watch you with great excitement as God continues to mold and shape you into powerful women of God.

To my father, who taught me the meaning of hope and consistency. To my mother, who taught me faithfulness and strength. I love you both very much.

And in memory of Jane Hill, who set a high Christian standard to follow and challenged me by her life to become God's woman.

Contents

‿

A Note from the Author

I vividly remember how exciting it was to receive and open the first case of *Liberated Through Submission* when it was originally published. One day shortly thereafter, my husband Frank and I got into what I call "intense fellowship." We had reached an impasse, and he ended our conversation by stating, "Go read your book!" I realized at that moment that I indeed had the concept of submission in my head, but it had not fully traveled to my heart. Over the years that journey has been made complete as I have watched God's continued faithfulness when exercising this principle. Today the power of submission burns even brighter in my heart.

Countless testimonies from men and women, single and married, concerning their victories when applying submission to their lives continue to abound. I have watched relationships restored that seemed doomed for destruction. I've seen strife replaced by peace and harmony. Truly God's ways are not our ways, and His thoughts are not our thoughts (Isaiah 55:8). Being liberated through submission may sound like a paradox, but I assure you it is the source of true freedom.

When this book was first released, my children were still at home. Today, the majority of them are adults, and I have had an opportunity to witness how the principle of submission flows into the next generation. My life has been richly blessed as I have observed them applying this principle to their careers and their jobs, in their churches and in their marriages. Oh, that parents would grasp the vision of how the future could be positively impacted if their children saw submission modeled correctly!

What about you? How do you view the principle of submission? Is it a positive or a negative? If your answer is positive, my desire is that this book will affirm that belief. If your answer is negative, I hope to reveal spiritual truths that will release you from the flawed teachings promoted by a world that hates God and by Satan, who has conspired to keep you from being set free.

Liberated Through Submission can make a tremendous, positive impact in your life and the lives of those around you...if you'll heed its message and apply its principles. Are you ready? Read on!

"I'm Never Getting Married!"

You can wait patiently for the Fourth of July to arrive to enjoy the brilliant fireworks. Or you can mention the word "submission" to a group of women! Their verbal response is likely to be just as explosive and colorful as any summer skyrockets or sparklers you could ever hope to see. Few words in the English language (or in any other language) evoke such a controversial response as the word "submission."

Before my conversion to Christianity, I was an atheist

with very little knowledge of the Word of God. Then one day, as a new Christian, I encountered a Scripture that said: "Wives, submit yourselves unto your own husbands, as unto the Lord" (Ephesians 5:22).

My first thought was, "Why would God mess up a good book with a Scripture like that?"

In my mind's eye, I suddenly pictured myself walking ten paces behind my husband, obediently dropping grapes into his mouth as he leisurely reclined, muzzling my opinions, and "ministering" to his every desire.

On the other hand, my husband, Frank, thought submission was a great idea! As a matter of fact, he often reminded me that many of our problems would simply dissolve if I would just submit and stop "challenging him."

In those days, when I thought of submission, only one other experience came close to matching my emotional response. That was the nauseating morning sickness that plagued me when I was pregnant!

Is God Unjust?

This wasn't the first time in my life that God had seemed unfair and unjust to me. Before I came to know Him, I often looked into the face of my blind, deformed sister Lizzie, mentally retarded and just eleven months older than I. How many times did I say to myself, "Surely no God of love would allow such a tragedy!" That kind of thinking led to my eventual conclusion that there was no God—period.

Over the years, I thought I had convinced myself that God didn't exist. But, in fact, I was forever interrogating people who believed in Him. My curiosity about their faith was relentless. Now I can see that I never really was an atheist. I was, instead, merely a person who accepted the easiest solution when unable to answer life's most difficult questions. Instead of submitting to His sovereignty, I had chosen to remove God from the picture!

Not long ago, as I was listening to my husband address a couples' conference, my mind wandered back to our first meeting. Frank was a friend of my sister Eleanor, and I got to know him while he tried to teach me to play tennis.

In those days Frank Wilson was moving rapidly up in the music industry as a record producer and writer. He was one of Motown's leading producers. He had written and produced such songs as "You've Made Me So Very Happy," "I'm Gonna Make You Love Me," "Love Child," and "Keep On Truckin'," which were recorded by stars like Diana Ross, Stevie Wonder and Blood, Sweat and Tears.

Frank's tunes had earned more than 20 gold and platinum records as well as several Grammy nominations. At the time we met, Frank had recently been the number-one record producer in much of Europe, number four in the United States, and "producer of the year."

One of the things that attracted me most to my husband was his humility in light of his success. Very down-to-earth and sensitive, he reminded me of my father, who had set a wonderful example of love for me in my early years. Within four weeks of my first date with Frank, we were married. (That, by the way, is something I wouldn't do today without premarital counseling!)

When Frank proposed, I told him I would marry him on one condition: that I would always be free to work outside the home. At that time, I was one of the first women sales representatives hired by Xerox. I had acquired the position with no former sales experience—unheard of at that major international corporation.

For months, I had been bound and determined to work for Xerox. Even though I'd been told by several people that I would never be hired, I'd made an appointment with the manager. Fortunately for me, the day I arrived for my interview, his secretary had just walked off the job. He reviewed my resumé. "Thank you," he said, "but I couldn't possibly hire you. You have absolutely no experience in sales!"

"Let me make you an offer," I said. "You've just lost your secretary, and that means your productivity is about to decrease. I'm one of the best secretaries you could ever find. Let me work for you for two weeks at minimum wage. At the end of two weeks, if you don't think I'll be an asset to your company as a sales representative, I won't darken your door again."

In two weeks, I was a sales representative for Xerox. I remained among their top-rated reps throughout my time with them. I can still remember how I enjoyed being a woman in a man's world. I was aggressive, determined and very outspoken. I had left home at 18 years old, moved 2500 miles away on my own and felt I had everything under control.

Then, the next thing I knew, I was in Las Vegas, beginning an all-new life as Frank Wilson's bride!

The early days of our marriage were challenging, to

say the least. Just a year after our marriage, I accepted Christ into my life and Frank recommitted his life to Him. Adjusting my mind to the mind of Christ was extremely painful, for I found myself yielding to Him some of my most-valued treasures: pride, contention, rebellion and stubbornness.

As a young wife and mother as well as a new Christian, I was intent upon discovering biblical solutions for everyday challenges. I found that intellectually and emotionally I was still having real difficulties with some of God's ways. This was particularly true in the area of submission. However, against my better judgment, I dove headlong into the "act" of submission anyway. My well-intentioned actions were derived from distorted concepts drawn from television shows, magazines and human observation.

I thought I was making good progress, moving forward at a steady pace. Then something unexpected happened.

The Wedding Gown

One day, while shopping in a mall near our home, I was drawn to a store window where an exquisite wedding gown was displayed. The hustle and bustle of all the people around me seemed to cease. I could almost hear an imaginary organ playing the wedding march! My mind raced forward about 20 years and I imagined my tiny daughter, Launi, gliding down a church aisle dressed in that lovely, white lace gown.

With a smile, I admiringly said to her, so pretty and

petite at my side, "Just think, one day you'll wear a beautiful dress like that."

"I'm never getting married!" Launi fumed.

I was outraged! How could a six-year-old make such a statement? Furthermore, how could *my* six-year-old make such a statement? My shocked reflection in the bridal shop window would have made Gloria Steinem jump to her feet in a standing ovation, shake her fist and shout the words, "I told you so!"

As I tried to absorb the incident, I thought perhaps Launi was just a little overtired from our long walk through the mall. But a second look at her quietly determined face told me she had given her outburst a considerable amount of thought.

My mind raced backward to my own childhood when I, too, had come to some definite conclusions relating to marriage. Until meeting my husband, I had been a confirmed bachelorette who'd never wanted to get married nor have children. Once I met Frank, however, I discovered attributes and characteristics in him I had not seen in any other man. I'd decided to take the plunge.

Now, fighting to regain my composure, I asked Launi to repeat what she had said. I was hoping she'd mixed up a few words. Fixing her eyes on mine, she firmly repeated, "I'm *never* getting married!"

Naturally, my next question was, "Why?"

Launi's response altered the course of my submissive life!

"Because I'm not going to have a man tell me what to do like Daddy tells you what to do. You have to ask him to do everything! You don't like it, and I won't either!"

I was reduced to a stammering, stuttering defense. "I don't ask Daddy everything," I insisted. "Why, I came to the mall today all by myself, and I didn't even ask him!"

The disgusted expression on her face was enough to tell me my portrait should hang in the Hall of Hypocrites.

So this was the end result of all my dutiful submission! I should have known it wouldn't work. This six-year-old had seen right through all my smiles and surrendering. I felt as if I had been hiding in a dark cave for years and had suddenly been jerked out into the startling sunlight.

Like Mother, Like Daughter

Another incident later that same day further chipped away at my submissive facade. As Launi walked through the kitchen, I reminded her to go upstairs and clean her room. Her shoulders dropped, her head flew back and out came a long sigh, "Oh, Mom!"

Angrily I reached for her shoulder, spun her around sharply and proclaimed, "Little girl, when I tell you to do something, not only do I want you to do it, but you had better do it with the right attitude!"

How resoundingly the Lord caused those words to echo in my soul! The right attitude? She'd seen me respond in the same way countless times before. Launi was simply acting like her mother!

I began to recall some little hints she had dropped before. Now and then she'd question me after Frank had asked me to do something. She would take my hand and inquire, "Mommy, are you mad?"

I would look at her a bit puzzled and wonder why she was asking me such a peculiar question. I didn't realize that, although I always put on an outward act of daily submission, she could see the resentment written all over my face.

Why Submission?

Inner questions began to surge like a flash flood. I asked myself, "If there is no giving in marriage in heaven, no male and female, why did God appoint the married woman to the unfair role of submission? Why did He give us females insight, intuitive abilities and intelligence if we aren't to use them?"

As tormenting as those questions were, I had been with the Lord long enough to know that Luke 11:9 was true:

> Ask, and it shall be given you;
> Seek, and ye shall find;
> Knock, and it shall be opened
> unto you.

So, ask I did! I began questioning scores of women. And the consistent, negative response to the question, "What do you think about submission?" could have made the *Guinness Book of World Records!* Some of the women honestly believed the Bible was correct and said, "Yes, one should submit." But they were submitting like I was—from the head and not the heart.

The Kitchen

Another occasion that jarred me into aggressively seeking more answers occurred in my kitchen during a visit with a close friend.

I adjusted the height of the flame under the chicken and began to stir the rice into the boiling water. And I noticed out of the corner of my eye that my friend was leaning against the kitchen counter with her arms folded.

She didn't appear to be tired from her cross-country journey. How immaculately dressed she was! Her manicured nails and neatly sculptured hairstyle reflected a woman of good standing in the business world. She had taken a break from her demanding schedule to come and relax with our family.

I turned my head toward her and saw her smiling. "What are you smiling about?" I couldn't help but ask.

"Oh, it just seems kind of amusing to see a real-life wife, in a real-life kitchen, stirring a real-life pot. I mean, you look like what I read about in books." There was a hint of sarcasm in her voice.

"Well," I answered with equal sarcasm, "it's a lousy job, but someone has to do it." Then I couldn't resist. I had to ask her the 50,000-dollar question. "Okay," I asked, "what's *your* opinion of submission?"

Although a Christian, my friend was newly saved. She dropped her hands to her sides, pushed herself away from the counter and became rigid, as if every nerve in her body had suddenly stood at attention. She stared at me with such defiance that it caused the hair to rise on the back of my neck. I dropped the spoon into the rice and marveled as she firmly retorted, "Submission was a custom of the Old Testament. It was a method to keep women oppressed and does not apply in the twentieth century or any other century to come!"

I was amazed at her angry, condescending response.

Once she left, I began to question God earnestly. Why are there so many unpleasant reactions to submission? Why the anger and rebellion?

I had always been impressed with such dynamic female leaders as Patricia Richardson, Vonette Bright and Beverly LaHaye. They had come to terms with the submission challenge—it was evident in their faces, words and actions. How I longed to know the truth behind this elusive principle. I somehow sensed that the essence of God's power was inherent in it!

Over a period of another four years, I found God ready, willing and able to answer me. But in stretching to cross the finish line of understanding, I had many "hurdles" to jump. Some heavy questions impeded my progress:

- Do I have to submit to everything my husband wants?

- Is submission for married women only?

- What if I have a higher education, a better job and make more money than the one in authority?

- Does submission mean that I'm not supposed to voice my opinions?

- When I'm positive that someone in authority has made the wrong decision, do I have any options?

As these and scores of other questions swirled in my

mind, I heard a story that focused my thinking once again on the real culprit behind our submission dilemma.

The Cockerpoo and the Pit Bull

While I rode to court with a fellow juror one day, he shared a true story with me. A man named Tom owned a full-grown cockerpoo (cocker spaniel and poodle mixed). Wanting a second dog, he bought a pit bull puppy which, at the time, fit into the palm of his hand.

The cockerpoo, of course, did not like sharing the limelight with the pit bull. It challenged the puppy and beat him up regularly. A pit bull, by the way, resembles a boxer in appearance and build, and is known to be a ferocious fighter, having tremendous strength in its jaws.

Surprisingly, even after the pit bull was fully grown and twice the size of the cockerpoo, the tiny dog with the big bark still ran the show.

One day, while the cockerpoo was romping around in the front yard, he became entangled in the garden hose, which happened to be turned on at the time. His thick coat became matted and tangled. When Tom took the cockerpoo in to be groomed, he was informed that it would be necessary to cut off all the dog's hair.

The next day, Tom returned to pick up his cockerpoo who could hardly wait to return to his domain. When they pulled up in front of the house, the cockerpoo jumped out and pranced proudly through the front door as if to announce, "The king is home!"

The pit bull, asleep in the corner, opened up one eye and then the other. He stood to his feet and stared at the skinny, hairless dog parading around the house. He did not recognize the cockerpoo! Can you guess what happened? Because the pit bull did not recognize him, he attacked and all but killed his former tormentor!

As I considered my concerns about submission, I could see that Satan is a defeated enemy who, like the cockerpoo, still tries to parade around as "the real thing." No matter how he tries to deceive, however, Jesus' power is available to us as we confront Satan in his masquerade!

In essence, this book has a twofold purpose: to reveal the tactics Satan uses to degrade and devalue the importance of submission, and to illustrate the power we can use to have victory over him.

There may be a tendency as you read to think, "If my spouse would just do this, I would do that...." I wish I had a dollar for every married woman who has told me, "I would submit to my husband if he would love me as Christ loves the church" or for every married man who has said, "If my wife would just submit, I'd be a better leader."

My children Tracey, Launi, Fawn and Christy Joy are a never-ending example of that kind of thinking. I can hardly ever remember hearing them respond to my correction with "Mom, you know, you're right. I was wrong. Please forgive me." What I usually hear is "You didn't say that to Fawn" or "What about Launi and Christy?" So often we point a reproachful finger at another person rather than take full responsibility for our own actions.

You'll soon see that, in the Garden of Eden, God did some questioning as to what had happened there. In response, Adam blamed Eve. Eve blamed the serpent.

The serpent slithered away in search of someone else to accuse.

You'll receive maximum benefit from this book if you think only of yourself and your own accountability as you read it. Don't forget that when we stand at the judgment to receive our rewards, we will be there all alone. Jesus said, "Behold, I am coming quickly, and My reward is with Me, to render to every man [or woman] according to what he [or she] has done" (Revelation 22:12 NASB).

In the meantime, rejoice! I'm about to share with you some wonderful principles I've learned. Through God's plan for submission, we can be released, not imprisoned. We can be freed, not enslaved. We can be exonerated, not condemned.

For far too long, women and men have been surrounded by myths and fallacies concerning submission, lies that have trapped their lives in frustration and rebellion. It is my deepest desire that you will begin to understand a glorious biblical principle that our loving God has bestowed upon us. It is my fervent prayer that you will become liberated—through submission.

Chapter 2

Mount Submission

‿

As I drove toward my home one brisk, windswept autumn morning, I was awed by the majestic mountains that surround Pasadena, California.

They appeared close enough to touch, and almost seemed to be singing "America the Beautiful," along with the clear, blue sky and puffy white clouds.

I looked at my three-year-old sitting next to me and exclaimed, "Christy, aren't those mountains beautiful?"

She sat up in her seat, stretched her neck to see out the front window, then turning to me said, "Where, Mommy?"

I thought she was joking until I saw the bewildered look on her face. "There—right in front of you," I replied.

"Where, Mommy?" she repeated.

Christy didn't know what a mountain was! My mind searched for a description and finally I asked, "Do you see those big piles of dirt in front of you?"

"No, Mommy," she replied.

"Do you see those things sticking up against the blue sky?" I tried again.

Christy scrunched her eyes, peered out the window and answered, "No, Mommy."

The mountains seemed to stop their singing as I helplessly tried one description after another. I thought all hope was lost when I rounded a corner just before reaching our home. There I caught sight of a mountaintop peeking over one of the houses facing me. I slammed on my brakes.

"Christy," I shrieked, "do you see the red car in the driveway in front of us?" She replied, "Yes."

"Do you see the house behind the red car?" I continued. She nodded her head up and down.

Anxiously I said, "Do you see that dirt sticking up behind the house?"

She exclaimed, "Yes!"

I shouted, *"Christy, that's a mountain!"*

We both giggled, sat back in our seats and breathed a sigh of relief.

Silly as that may seem, God had to do the same thing

with me when it came to submission. For me, the principle of submission was much like those mountains. It was so big that it surrounded every relationship, situation and circumstance in life. Yet it is not unusual to hear a person say, as I did, "I can't see or understand submission. It's hard for me to get a handle on it." It's as if a dense fog shrouds its existence.

Like Christy, I once sat with God, scrunching my eyes, trying to see the mountain. He was kind enough to point out some basic principles that ultimately led me to a deeper understanding of submission—the essence of His power.

Principle #1:
Submission Is for Everyone

When speaking to groups, I usually observe some interesting body language when I first mention the word "submission." The men relax, lean back in their chairs and smile. They are so *very* grateful that a woman has appeared to set some things straight!

The single people shrug their shoulders, stare out into space and start thinking about something they feel is relevant to them.

The married women stiffen, dig their nails into the palms of their hands and grit their teeth. They are polite, but resentful of being subjected to such an inapplicable and misdirected issue.

It usually comes as a shock to most audiences when they learn that submission is for everyone. We are *all* called to submit!

Submitting yourselves one to another
(Ephesians 5:21).

Yea, all of you be subject one to another,
and be clothed with humility; for God resisteth
the proud, and giveth grace to the humble
(1 Peter 5:5).

Now, be honest. When was the last time you heard
someone say, "He's a submissive man" or "She's such a
submissive single woman"? Popularly speaking, "submissive" is not a term used to describe either men or single
individuals.

Ironically, most of us don't know why. So subtle has
been the propaganda, we don't even know how we reached
the conclusion that submission applies to married women
only. We have conformed to the world's concept, accepting
its views. We have become all-too-comfortable, costuming
ourselves and acting out roles that God never intended
for us.

The Gorilla

One day a man with a great deal of debt and responsibility lost his job. Frantically, he began to search the
newspaper for employment. In the corner of the second
page he read, "Popular Gorilla Dies at Local Zoo." He
tucked the paper under his arm and made a mad dash
for the zoo.

Upon arriving, the man located the manager, ran up
to him, grabbed his arm and said, "Look, I just read that
you've lost your most popular animal here in the zoo."

The startled manager nodded his head sadly.

"Well, I have an idea," the man continued. "You need a gorilla and I need a job. Why don't you let me get a gorilla suit and fill in the spot. I'll do it for a week without pay. If it works out, I'll have a job and you'll have a gorilla!"

The manager pushed his hat to the back of his head, cocked one eyebrow and mumbled as he walked away, "Go ahead and give it a try."

Would you believe the man was a colossal hit the very first week? The crowds were bigger than ever before. He loved it! He amused them with myriad tricks. One day the gorilla noticed a rope hanging in his cage. He climbed up on a ledge and swung out across the cage. The people cheered and threw popcorn in the air.

The next day the gorilla decided to be more daring. He opened his cage door and swung out over the lion's cage. The lion roared and leaped frantically toward the gorilla.

The onlookers shouted with excitement!

This became one of the gorilla's favorite tricks. But as fate would have it, the day came when he swung out across the lion's cage and the rope broke. The gorilla fell flat on his face in front of the lion. When he raised his head, he was looking straight down the lion's mouth. He jumped to his feet and started screaming, "Help! Help!"

The lion quickly leaped in front of him and said in a low female voice, "Quiet dummy, or we'll both lose our jobs!"

We people are not so different from the lion and the gorilla.

We clothe ourselves in mental and emotional disguises,

defying anyone to know who we are. Some of us have dressed that way for so long, we've begun to believe in the fictitious characters we're portraying.

The first time I unzipped my costume and stood in the light of God's Word to find out who I was, I was very uncomfortable. Then I learned that God had something of His own He wanted me to wear. I found out about it in Matthew 11:28-30:

> Come unto me, all ye that labour and are heavy laden, I will give you rest. Take my yoke upon you, and learn of me; for I am meek and lowly in heart; and ye shall find rest unto your souls. For my yoke is easy, and my burden is light.

How free, how truly liberated we are when we live our lives God's way!

It might be different if we had to deal with submission only every now and then. However, there's very little time in the course of a day when we are not challenged to "yield pleasantly" or to submit to God's Word. It happens in nearly every area of our lives.

God's Principle

After Oprah Winfrey read this book, she invited Frank and me to be featured guests on her program. I was nervous, thinking about addressing 20 million people on submission! But, encouraged by the Holy Spirit, we went anyway. We found ourselves interacting with four soon-to-be-married couples, and a studio audience packed with engaged couples.

Preceding both that appearance and our interview on CBN's "Heart to Heart" with Sheila Walsh, we had requested that surveys be conducted of random groups of people. The groups represented a broad spectrum of races, cultures and religions. The question was asked, "What do you think of when you hear the word 'submission'?"

The answers were invariably negative. Most people felt that submission was synonymous with being subservient or inferior. The general impression was that a person would be treated like a "doormat" if he were submissive. It was especially startling to find that both Christians and non-Christians shared the same thoughts.

If you were to ask a group of Christians, "Do you think Jesus was a wimp?" what do you think the response would be? They would probably complain that you'd asked the most absurd question they'd ever heard. Yet Jesus Christ led a totally submissive life: "The Father hath not left me alone; for I do always those things that please him" (John 8:29).

As we follow in His footsteps, by operating according to an established order, those who look upon our lives may want to challenge our decisions. From the outside, we may give every appearance of being a doormat. The statements, "You need to stand up and fight!" or "Are you going to let them walk all over you?" will become commonplace. However, from the inside we will have the assurance that the God who intervened on behalf of Jesus is also handling our case.

Many times Jesus was reviled and did not revile back.

He was insulted, cursed at and humiliated, always without retaliation. Ultimately, He died at the hands of His tormentors. And He died willingly. Why then do we think of Him as being powerful?

It is because we know the end of the story!

We know that He rose from the grave with all power in His nail-scarred hands. Jesus understood the strength contained in the principle of submission. And Scripture exhorts us: "Let this mind be in you, which was also in Christ Jesus" (Philippians 2:5).

During the "Oprah Winfrey Show," I was asked the question, "Bunny, why did you entitle your book *Liberated Through Submission?*"

I responded, "Because, Oprah, that's what has liberated and set me free."

She then asked, "What does 'submission' mean?"

" 'Submission,' " I responded, "means what the dictionary says it means. It means to yield—yield to people, precepts and principles that have been placed in our lives as authorities. Throughout our lives, someone is always in authority. At home it's our parents; in school, the teacher or principal. In business it's our employer and at church it's our pastor."

I proceeded to paint a picture of what submission looks like. "Imagine for a moment that there are two vehicles traveling down a freeway. On the right is a semitrailer truck and on the left a compact car. The vehicles travel side by side for 15 minutes or so. Then a sign appears indicating that the two lanes must merge into one.

"Based on the *position* of the truck, it has to yield to the compact car. The semi is stronger, bigger and more powerful. It could force its way. But if it did, there would be a collision. And so the semi truck yields to the compact car, and they progressively move down the freeway until the lanes open up and they are side by side once again."

After a friend of ours watched the program and heard my metaphor, he said to me, "I don't think you should have said I was a compact and my wife was a semi truck!" After we stopped laughing, I went on to explain to him that the semi truck represents the strong feelings, opinions and emotions we experience when we do not agree with someone in authority—male *or female.*

An Established Order

Submission does not just belong to Christians. It is a universal principle, much like the law of gravity or the rule of reaping what you sow. Whether in your church, home, country or business, yielding and operating according to an established order results in greater peace.

When we begin a new job, one of the first things we want to know is to whom we are answerable. We begin to immediately establish an order in which we will be able to effectively function. A sharp executive will quickly produce a flow chart for his business, and much of his success will depend on who holds strategic positions of power.

In any business, once authority has been established, those exerting control usually have a certain mind-set. The person in charge does not stand over an underling to make sure his work is complete. Employee suggestions are usually welcomed. However, in cases where they are not accepted, the employee is still expected to maintain a good and courteous attitude and to move forward agreeably, submitting to the final decision.

We understand the concept of working according to an established order in business. But often there is a struggle when we attempt to apply it to our homes and churches. This is curious, since yielding to leadership makes the most sense when exercised under the ultimate authority of Christ. Submission most certainly works best when faith is part of the equation.

Principle #2:
Submission Plus Faith
Equals Power

Submission without faith is slavery. Submission with faith is power! It takes faith to believe that God is correcting a relationship, situation or circumstance when all outward signs show the opposite. "For we walk by faith, not by sight" (2 Corinthians 5:7).

Throughout the Bible we are admonished by God to submit (be subject) to those who are in authority:

Everyone must submit to God.

> Submit yourselves therefore to God (James 4:7).

Everyone must submit to church leadership.

> Obey them that have the rule over you, and submit yourselves; for they watch for your souls, as they that must give account, that they may do it with joy, and not with

grief; for this is unprofitable for you (Hebrews 13:17).

Everyone must submit to authorities in the land.

> Submit yourselves to every ordinance of man for the Lord's sake; whether it be to the king, as supreme; or unto governors, as unto them that are sent by him for the punishment of evildoers, and for the praise of them that do well. For so is the will of God (1 Peter 2:13-15).

Everyone must submit to employers.

> Servants, be submissive to your masters with all respect, not only to those who are good and gentle, but also to those who are unreasonable (1 Peter 2:18 NASB).

Wives must submit to husbands.

> Wives, submit yourselves unto your own husbands, as unto the Lord (Ephesians 5:22).

Whether we are men or women, when those in authority disagree with us, we have the right to express our differing opinions in love. In fact, I believe we have a responsibility to communicate our thoughts and ideas, "speaking the truth in love" (Ephesians 4:15), and should do so whenever possible. But our attitude is to be one of humility, and the final decision is to be theirs!

And what if we're absolutely, positively sure we're right? What if we know that their decision will have a negative effect on the church, job or home? At that point we have to make a choice. We can respond by continuing to press our point and force the issue, which will often result in anger and strife, or we can turn to Philippians 2:14,15:

> Do all things without murmurings and disputings: That ye may be blameless and harmless, the sons of God, without rebuke in the midst of a crooked and perverse nation, among whom ye shine as lights in the world.

So do we just give up? No! That would be stopping too short. We are to give up, but give the situation up *to God!* God is the equalizing factor in all situations. We must choose to go against our human nature, which insists we get our own way. Then, once we've chosen to exercise faith in our situation, God's power is unleashed.

Sometimes He resolves the issue quickly; other times, patience will be required on our part to see the situation settled. And we must always keep in mind that the other person just may be right. If so, God will reveal that, also.

Just how does God deal with people who are in authority and choose to go contrary to our suggestions? We find the answer in Proverbs 21:1: "The king's heart is in the hand of the Lord, as the rivers of water; he turneth it whithersoever he will."

The *Matthew Henry Commentary* explains it this way:

> Even the hearts of men are in God's hand. God can change men's minds, can turn them from that which they seemed most intent upon, as the husbandman, by canals and gutters, turns the water through his grounds, which does not alter the nature of the water, nor put any force upon it, any more than God's providence does upon man's will, but directs the course of it to serve his own purpose.[1]

God would love to fix the relationships, situations and circumstances in our lives because we are His children and He loves us. However, we are the ones that prevent His action. We tie His hands with cords of rebellion and stubbornness. In the Old Testament we read:

> For rebellion is as the sin of witchcraft,
> and stubbornness is as iniquity and idolatry
> (1 Samuel 15:23).

When we defy people placed in authority, we are really saying that the situation cannot be resolved unless we take action. We are, in actual fact, playing God.

When we go to God and say, "Father, I think this person is wrong, but I'm trusting you to show him (or her) what's right and to change them," that simple act of faith releases His power to freely act on our behalf. We can also pray, "Lord, if in their stubbornness they refuse

---

1. Reverend Leslie F. Church, Ph.D., ed., *Matthew Henry Commentary* (Grand Rapids, MI: Zondervan, 1961), p. 770.

to submit to Your guidance, I know I can count on you to rectify the outcome, no matter what!"

> Humble yourselves therefore under the mighty hand of God, that he may exalt you in due time (1 Peter 5:6).

Once we've committed the issue to God, our faith in Him liberates us to be around the opposing person without murmuring and strife. If the other individual is wrong, God begins to show that person in ways only known to Him. Perhaps, while we're sleeping soundly eight hours every night, the other man or woman is tossing and turning in a rumpled bed.

It takes childlike faith to believe that God can handle any person, debate or circumstance. When we choose to submit, we can easily see why God says that unless we become as little children we cannot enter the kingdom of God.

Principle #3:
Submission Plus Power
Equals Liberation

It may be that, at the moment, you're feeling frustrated with certain people in your life. Or you're annoyed about tensions that have arisen over disagreements. Or you're feeling troubled about the outcome of situations in which you had to relinquish control. Could a subtle attitude of rebellion be creeping into your thoughts?

If so, consider Jesus. He is always our best example of submission at work. We know that He often slipped away to pray to His Father. Do you think that He went only to receive orders about what He was to do next? Mark 14:36 reveals that Jesus both shared His heart and also surrendered to the Father's final authority.

> Abba, Father, all things are possible unto thee; take away this cup from me; nevertheless not what I will, but what thou wilt.

Jesus knew all too well about the suffering He would soon face on the cross. He questioned the means His Father had chosen for man's salvation, yet He submitted Himself to the Father's final decision. It's an awesome lesson in submission to realize that our personal salvation rested upon Jesus' submission.

What We Don't Know Can Hurt Us

A judge once said, "Ignorance of the law does not release us from the penalty of the law."

Suppose you are traveling through some out-of-state town and driving 35 MPH. You're stopped by a policeman who informs you that the speed limit is 25 MPH. I doubt seriously that he would accept "Sorry, sir. I didn't know" as an excuse.

And if you decided to fight the ticket and stood before the judge with the excuse, "I didn't know the speed limit," you can be pretty sure what the judge's answer would be: "If you are driving, it's your responsibility to know the speed limit."

Many of us have spent our lives violating God's principle of submission. We have received a steady stream of tickets, and we have no idea how or where to pay them. Some of our tickets are so old that they have turned into warrants, leaving us imprisoned in our rebellion and stubbornness.

And suppose you disagree with a pastor, employer or in the case of wives, a husband, and you are given a chance to present your case in court. The judge has reviewed both sides of the case and agrees with you. You are seated in front of the judge while the person you disagree with is standing to argue his position.

As the other person presents his case, you become upset. You jump to your feet, screaming in defense of yourself. What does the judge do? Even if he agrees with you, he says, "You are out of order! If you don't sit down you will be held in contempt of court." People who have not otherwise broken the law have actually been sent to jail for exhibiting this kind of disrespect.

Many Christians are living their lives in contempt of God because they refuse to surrender to an order that God, not man, has established.

We may sometimes ask, "What if the people I submit to make mistakes? I'm the one who's going to suffer the consequences of their actions!" The answer to that is, once again, faith.

Being human, we all make mistakes—a fact which should keep us from pointing a finger at someone else and saying, "I told you so." A spirit of love shown to one in error will allow him (or her) to regroup. And the next time you share an opinion, you can believe that it will be heard more attentively. Many of us want to force our ideas on people in authority without having earned the right.

We can believe, by faith, that God can heal someone of cancer, free someone of a drug addiction, or place a child in a barren womb. But do we have the faith to believe that God can speak to another person's heart and tell him what to do? Do we believe that God can make the best of a situation, even when an authority figure blindly opposes God's directions?

These questions are true tests of faith. Do you have the confidence to believe that God can fix anything? There's an old saying: "God can hit a straight line with a crooked stick."

Are you beginning to see that submission, like that mountain I showed Christy, entirely surrounds our lives? Through submission we can ascend to the top of the mountain and soar over challenges like a magnificent eagle. We cannot physically see the air that holds the eagle in the sky. In the same way, we cannot physically see the hand of God, holding and controlling every heart and every situation.

We can't see God's hand, but it's there!

Chapter 3

Lost in the Garden

Every now and then one of my children comes running to me, upset and crying. Before she attempts to sputter out the details of her dilemma, I always say, "Hold it! Let's start from the beginning." In order to fully understand most anything, that seems to be the very best place to start!

Like everything else, there was a point in time when submission began. It started all the way back in Genesis.

> Adam and Eve were meant to please
> A God who loved them so
> But Adam and Eve accepted the tease
> And God said they'd have to go
> Now you and me, like Adam and Eve
> Must face a life of woe.

God created man after His image and in His own likeness. The garden story reveals everything we need to know about God's purpose, plan and position relating to the principle of submission. Follow along carefully and you will see the magnificent wisdom of the God we serve.

> And the Lord God formed man from the dust of the ground and breathed into his nostrils the breath of life, and man became a living being. Now the Lord God had planted a garden in the east, in Eden; and there he put the man he had formed. And the Lord God made all kinds of trees grow out of the ground—trees that were pleasing to the eye and good for food. In the middle of the garden were the tree of life and the tree of the knowledge of good and evil.... The Lord God took the man and put him in the Garden of Eden to work it and take care of it. And the Lord God commanded the man, "You are free to eat from any tree in the garden; but you must not eat from the tree of the knowledge of good and evil, for when you eat of it you will surely die" (Genesis 2:7-9, 15-17).

A Big Question

Whenever I read this particular passage of Scripture, I recall a childhood incident that seems as if it happened just yesterday! I remember sitting across the desk from our elderly minister, kicking my feet against the bottom of a chair and staring at the cracks in the ceiling of his office. After I sighed a few times, he stopped reading his book and peered at me over the top of his glasses. When he began to speak, I wondered if God sounded like that. My anticipation began to build. Maybe, at long last, someone would be able to answer my big question.

"Little girl," he began, "I understand that you have a question that no one seems to have an answer for."

I pushed forward to the end of my chair and nodded. I replied, "That's right, sir."

Hesitating for just a moment, I took a deep breath and blurted out, "I just can't understand how a good God could put a bad tree in the middle of a good garden! I mean, if He's all good, how could He even think up a bad tree?"

The minister looked past me to my Sunday school teacher and smiled patronizingly. My anticipation turned to anger. It was evident that he, just like the teacher who had brought me to see him, thought it was a silly question.

He leaned back in his chair and uttered four words slowly: "Have faith in God."

That was the most ridiculous answer I had ever heard in my 11 years on earth! When I opened my mouth to ask another question, he raised the palm of his hand, just like a traffic cop. "That's all, young lady," he said decisively.

One week later, I was expelled from Sunday school for

disturbing the class—and the teacher! The experience has haunted me ever since.

Now, all these years later, I think I understand a little better. God created Adam as a free moral agent with the ability to make decisions. God could have created him like a robot, walking around the garden all day saying, "Praise the Lord! Hallelujah! Thank You, God!" But God longed for Adam to love Him because he wanted to, not because it was demanded. And how could Adam make a choice if he had no options?

Suppose Frank and I were stranded on a lonely, tropical island, where every day he professed his loyalty to me. It wouldn't mean anything until a boat washed ashore and off stepped 20 raving beauties. Then his loyalty would mean something!

Notice that God put the tree of the knowledge of good and evil in the *middle* of the garden. Adam had to pass it often. The Scripture says the tree was pleasant to look at and its fruit could be eaten. So whenever Adam approached the tree, he had a decision to make. It must have pleased God every time Adam chose obedience to Him instead of the knowledge of good and evil.

A Helpmate for Adam

But then God decided to bless Adam with a companion.

> And the Lord God caused a deep sleep to fall upon Adam, and he slept; and he took one of his ribs, and closed up the flesh instead thereof; and the rib, which the Lord God had

taken from man, made he a woman, and brought her unto the man. And Adam said, This is now bone of my bones, and flesh of my flesh; she shall be called Woman, because she was taken out of Man....And they were both naked, the man and his wife, and were not ashamed (Genesis 2:21-25).

I'd like to draw your attention to the next two verses.

Now the serpent was more subtle than any beast of the field which the Lord God had made. And he said unto the woman, Yea, hath God said, Ye shall not eat of every tree of the garden? (Genesis 3:1).

There is no indication of the time lapse between Genesis 2:25 and 3:1, we can only imagine what must have been the greatest human love story ever told. Undoubtedly, those early days Adam and Eve spent together were a romanticist's dream come true.

Can you picture what it must have been like when God left the two of them standing alone in the garden for the first time? In my imagination, I can see them. Turning to face each other, their eyes met. They knew they were the same and yet very different. The garden which Adam simply continued to tend and keep beautiful now became their wonderland.

I can see Adam escorting Eve around the garden and introducing her to the various trees and flowers. And when he told her that he had named every animal in the garden, she must have turned and looked at him in amazement. In her eyes he saw something that he'd never seen before: admiration.

I envision them running across meadows hand in hand, jumping into bubbling streams that flowed through the garden. Their picnics had no menacing ants. Every animal was a friend. Their laughter would fly on the wings of doves. Their relationship was void of fear, jealousy, anger and strife—truly made in heaven. Every moment brought them closer and closer together.

And then the plot began to thicken. Then came that fatal day when Eve stood face to face with the serpent.

The Intruder

> The woman said unto the serpent, We may eat of the fruit of the trees of the garden; but of the fruit of the tree which is in the midst of the garden, God hath said, Ye shall not eat of it, neither shall ye touch it, lest ye die. And the serpent said unto the woman, Ye shall not surely die; for God doth know that in the day ye eat thereof, then your eyes shall be opened and ye shall be as gods, knowing good and evil. And when the woman saw that the tree was good for food, and that it was pleasant to the eyes, and a tree to be desired to make one wise, she took of the fruit thereof, and did eat, and gave also unto her husband with her; and he did eat (Genesis 3:2-6).

Something very interesting unfolds in these Scriptures. Did you notice Eve's response to the serpent when he told her that she would not surely die? Without so much as a question, she partook of the tree!

You'd think, when the serpent told Eve something totally contradictory to what she knew God had commanded Adam, she would have been shocked! I would have expected her to say, "That's incredible! That's nothing like what my husband told me and we're very close. I'm going to ask him about it."

Yet, without conferring with Adam, she ate of the fruit.

Logical Adam had refused to eat the forbidden fruit solely because God told him not to. Curious Eve couldn't help but wonder what it might be like to know the difference between good and evil. Satan gave her opportunity to find out, and she bit. The rest is, literally, history.

> And the eyes of them both were opened, and they knew that they were naked; and they sewed fig leaves together, and made themselves aprons. And they heard the voice of the Lord God walking in the garden in the cool of the day; and Adam and his wife hid themselves from the presence of the Lord God among the trees of the garden. And the Lord God called unto him, Where art thou? And he said, I heard thy voice in the garden, and I was afraid, because I was naked; and I hid myself. And he said, Who told thee that thou wast naked? Hast thou eaten of the tree, whereof I commanded thee that thou

shouldest not eat? And the man said, The
woman whom thou gavest to be with me,
she gave me of the tree and I did eat. And
the Lord God said unto the woman, What
is this that thou hast done? And the woman
said, The serpent beguiled me, and I did eat
(Genesis 3:7-13).

The Bible says that Adam was with her, yet he said
nothing. Eve really believed the serpent was telling the
truth. Adam knew very well that the serpent was lying:
"And Adam was not deceived, but the woman being
deceived was in the transgression" (1 Timothy 2:14).

When Adam saw Eve eat the forbidden fruit, he had
a decision to make. Would he live eternally without the
woman he loved or die with her? He chose to die.

Different Chastisements

At this point, submission ceased to be a matter of
loving understanding between the Creator and His
creation. Instead it became the basis of God's chastisement upon man and woman.

And the Lord God said unto the serpent,
Because thou hast done this, thou art cursed
above all cattle, and above every beast of the
field; upon thy belly shalt thou go, and dust
shalt thou eat all the days of thy life....Unto
the woman he said, I will greatly multiply
thy sorrow and thy conception; in sorrow
thou shalt bring forth children; and thy desire
shall be to thy husband, and he shall rule

over thee. And unto Adam he said, Because thou hast hearkened unto the voice of thy wife, and hast eaten of the tree, of which I commanded thee, saying, Thou shalt not eat of it; cursed is the ground for thy sake; in sorrow shalt thou eat of it all the days of thy life (Genesis 3:14-17).

Now I'd like to point out something significant. Although Adam and Eve committed the same sin, their punishments were totally different. That seems strange until we remember that God is our Father.

In our home, Frank and I do not chastise our children "just to be mean." We do it because we love them. We want to see their characters shaped in such a way that they will be able to lead productive and happy adult lives. Our chastisements usually consist of taking things away (TV, telephone privileges or special outings), or giving them things they would rather not have (gardening, cleaning, washing responsibilities). We believe that, through these forms of discipline, they will be reminded of what they did wrong and choose not to do it again. And since each of our children is different, what we take away or give depends upon the personality of the child.

God chastised Eve in two ways: by giving her something she did not want and by taking away the one thing she desired. First of all, God allowed Eve pain in childbirth. It was God's desire that Eve produce children and multiply the population of the earth, which should have been a wonderful experience. Instead, it became painful.

The second chastisement was the loss of something that was very important to Eve: control. She really believed when she ate the fruit that she would become like God. And so God said to Eve, "And *thy desire shall be* to thy husband and he shall rule over thee."

My husband once asked what I thought God meant when He said, "And thy desire shall be to thy husband."

After some thought, I smiled and responded. "I think we are cursed to want you. Even when we don't want you, we want you!"

He laughed and said, "I think there's more to it than that." He went on to explain the meaning of "desire for" in Genesis 4:7. In Genesis 4, we find the story of Cain and Abel, the sons of Adam and Eve. The brothers had offered up a sacrifice to God. He had accepted Abel's but rejected Cain's gift. Cain became upset and in verse 7, God responds by saying:

> If thou doest well, shalt thou not be accepted? And if thou doest not well, sin lieth at the door. And unto thee *shall be his desire* and thou shalt rule over him.

The word "desire" is the same one found in Genesis 3:16. What was "sin's desire" for Cain? To influence and control the course of his life.

When God cursed Eve, it was almost as if He said to her, "Okay, Eve. You want to be the boss and make the decisions? When you leave this garden you will always want to control and lead the course of your husband's life. But he will rule over you instead!"

Women, wait a minute before you stand up and shout,

"That's not true!" Consider a statement commonly made by women, Christian and non-Christian alike. I believe it is a garden conversation instituted by Eve and passed on through the generations. The statement is, "I need a strong man!" Have you ever heard a woman say, "I need a wimp"? But if you were to hear the rest of the sentence, it would go like this, "I need a strong man because if he is not strong, I'll walk all over him!"

A woman innately knows her desire to control. She longs to find a man who will take charge. It's unlikely she'll find one unless he is submitted to God's Word. The unlikelihood comes from the punishment God rendered to Adam.

Remember, Adam was in charge of keeping the garden manicured and beautiful. He would meet with God in the cool of the evening and the two of them would fellowship. I think it is safe to say that Adam had a relaxing life. When God punished Adam, He took away the leisure time and replaced it with hard work.

It was almost as if God said, "Okay, Adam. You've shown me that you don't want to make decisions or do what's right. So from now on, if you're going to eat, you'll first have to till the ground, plant the seed, water and fertilize it, wait for it to grow and harvest it! You will provide for yourself and your family by the sweat of your brow.

"Worst of all, you must rule over a woman who has proven, by making her own independent decision in the garden, that she will not be ruled. I know you'd rather relax, but you're going to have to take a leadership role, anyway!"

Now the men are shouting, "That's not true!" But let's once again consider a statement often made by men, Christian and non-Christian alike. The wife says to him, "I just don't think you love me anymore. I can't put my finger on it, but there is something different."

The man grumbles back, "What do you mean I don't love you? I go to work, don't I?"

Okay, men, could you please explain to me what going to work has to do with love? Deep inside, a man is really saying, "If it wasn't for you, I would be lying next to the Crystal River, naming the animals and dressing the garden. I don't want to go to work. And if I go, I go only because I love you!"

When you pay close attention, you'll notice that man, for the most part, is a professional relaxer. Even if he works hard, it's usually so he can retire early or buy higher-priced toys. Even the workaholic is often using his work addictively, and is not actually motivated simply because the work itself is rewarding. He may even be using it as an anesthetic, to mask some pain or fear. And even though some men work hard and receive applause and gratification from their labor, they still may not be true leaders in the home—the most difficult job of all.

If you want to see *real* contentment, watch a man the next time he's at a sporting event or fishing. I once went through four issues of *Field and Stream* magazine. There was not one woman in any of the advertisements! And I have yet to hear a single protest from anyone. Husbands usually have to say, "Honey, why don't you sit down and relax?" They don't understand that we don't have time to relax. (It takes a lot of energy to stay in control!)

So it is—with few exceptions—that women want to control and men want to relax. And it's not our fault! We got it from the garden. Well, let's say it's not our fault that we were *born* that way. But it is our fault if we stay that way.

Poor Adam, who had known no stress, now had to rule over Eve. He had to become responsible for a woman who proved by eating the fruit without discussion that she was, to say the least, a free-thinking, independent individual! Prior to the fall, God was the decision maker, and Adam and Eve had experienced no dissension in their relationship. Up until then, all had been pure and lovely.

Barred from their beautiful garden home, what culture shock they must have experienced! Leading was painstakingly difficult for Adam. Submitting was foreign to Eve. Neither of them wanted the responsibility God had placed on them. And I'm sure they both found it a bitter pill to submit to God's firm decision.

A New Way of Life

What was once the greatest human love story the world had ever known was about to become the greatest tragedy. And in a way I suppose it was a comedy, too. If "I Love Lucy" was funny, I'm sure "I Love Eve" was hilarious.

Can't you see Adam and Eve waking up the day after they were evicted from the garden? They turned to look at each other, and let's not forget that toothpaste and mouthwash had not been invented yet. When Adam said, "Good morning, Eve," her eyes crossed and she grabbed the animal skin and put it over her mouth before she said, "Good morning, Adam."

It wasn't long before they figured out that if they were going to eat, Adam would have to till the ground. Being a creature of habit himself, Adam, on his way to the field, probably greeted his favorite mountain lion with, "Hi there, friend!" I'm sure his screams could probably be heard for miles around as his old feline friend-turned-foe, chased him off into the hills.

After a long day's work, Adam was relieved to get home to Eve. He walked into their cave and said, "Hi, honey. What's for dinner?"

Eve glared at him and replied, "Dinner? I've been cleaning the cave all day. If you want dinner, fix it yourself!"

In the garden, Adam's bride hadn't had dishes to wash or meals to prepare. Now her days were spent cleaning and cooking while Adam was out raising their food. The sweet fragrance that had once surrounded them in the garden was replaced by dusty sweat and salty tears.

Eve truly was the mother of us all. She had to pioneer everything. There was no one to give her advice when she was pregnant with her babies or to warn her about childbirth. Her heart broke over the first murder when her son Cain killed his brother Abel. Her anguish could be felt again and again as she reflected back on what she had left in the garden with God. She and Adam carried the weight of their mistakes on their shoulders for the rest of their lives.

But the most continuing difficulty lay in the fact that Adam and Eve were forced to accept roles alien to them.

And the difficulty continues. If the Lord called a moratorium tomorrow and switched the roles of men and women, the country would have to declare a state of emergency! Would there be riots in the streets, with men and women fighting to maintain their established roles? No!

Women would be crowding the boardrooms nationwide, trying to clean up the mess they believed men had left for them. Meanwhile, the freeways would be full of men in cars, slowly moving along in bumper-to-bumper traffic, cheering and celebrating. Would they be on their way to Washington, D.C. to march on the White House in order to regain their rights? Quite to the contrary! The men would be on their way fishing, bowling, skiing, surfing, swimming, golfing, or off to play basketball, football, soccer or tennis!

Am I exaggerating? Perhaps a little. But we need to come to grips with the fact that men don't want to submit to God in leading their homes. And women don't want to submit to God in following their husbands. One is just as difficult as the other.

My husband has often told me that if it weren't for women, men would probably attain very little. A man is driven to accomplishment by the appreciation and admiration of a woman. And women by nature, like Eve, are curious, compelling and compulsive creatures. Female influence, as witnessed in the garden, has rippled throughout the pages of human history.

Woman was created to be man's helpmate. That means she should be an integral part of her husband's life, enabling him to fully develop into the kind of man

God wants him to be. This automatically makes her the kind of woman God wants her to be.

Even in our fallen state, that plan remains intact. However, without some very specific guidelines—husbands lead, wives submit—our sinful natures will cause us to make adjustments to God's sovereign plan. The result is the same as from the beginning: self-destruction.

Chapter 4

Submission and the Married Man

Being a man is tough! Being a Christian married man is overwhelming! Before I discovered that everyone is called to submit, including the married man, I was sure that God's justice scale was tipped in favor of men. Now that I know what they've been called to do, I'm surprised there hasn't been an uprising, complete with picket signs reading, "I Should Have Been Born a Woman!"

Ironically, there has been such an emphasis on submission among married women that the responsibilities of men have gone virtually unmentioned. Nevertheless, God has given men some very specific leadership assignments which, when accomplished, glorify His kingdom. But it takes a man surrendered to God's Word to carry out God's orders.

As we learned in Chapter 3, a woman does not want to follow and a man does not want the responsibility of family leadership. The Bible is filled with stories of men who were constantly running or hiding from God's directions. Only a man infused with God's Spirit takes the lead properly.

Many men greatly oppose the statement that they don't want to lead. They immediately cite their roles of leadership at work, in sports and in many other areas. However, there are very few men who will admit that they're under God's leadership, and even fewer who act that leadership out in the home. Why? Based on Adam's decision in the garden, a man does not want to govern his wife or home. His rebellion in that area is often justified and overshadowed by his outstanding achievements in other areas.

I've always considered myself a logical person. In recent years, I've dropped my defenses and examined submission from God's point of view. I have since concluded that if anyone has a right to complain to God (we don't, of course) about what He's called us to do, it would definitely be the married man. Let me share with you how an ex-atheist and ex-feminist came to that unlikely conclusion.

When God assigned Adam and Eve their roles as they left the garden, He didn't give them their complete job description until later. One of the most vivid descriptions is found in Ephesians 5:22-28:

> Wives, submit yourselves unto your own husbands, as unto the Lord. For the husband is the head of the wife, even as Christ is the head of the church; and he is the saviour of the body. Therefore, as the church is subject unto Christ, so let the wives be to their own husbands in everything. Husbands, love your wives, even as Christ also loved the church, and gave himself for it; that he might sanctify and cleanse it with the washing of water by the word, that he might present it to himself a glorious church, not having spot, or wrinkle, or any such thing; but that it should be holy and without blemish. So ought men to love their wives as their own bodies. He that loveth his wife loveth himself.

We find one other job description for the man in 1 Peter 3:7:

> Likewise, ye husbands, dwell with them according to understanding, giving honour unto the wife, as unto the weaker [more delicate] vessel, and as being heirs together of the grace of life; that your prayers not be hindered.

Now let's take a closer look at what we've just read. Before we examine each part separately, I want to list the responsibilities of the married man:

The Husband

1. Be the head (final decision maker) of the wife.
2. Love your wife.
3. Be the spiritual leader of your home.
4. Live with your wife according to understanding. (Understanding why and how God made her.)

The Wife

1. Wives, submit yourselves unto your own husbands as unto the Lord.

That's it! All wives are called to do is submit to their husbands! Meanwhile, their husbands are expected to yield to God's plan by being the head of the house, by loving their wives, by being the spiritual leader in the home and by living with a wife in an understanding way. God assigned him four times as much work!

Up a Tree!

This makes me think of a story about two men who escaped from prison late one night. Shortly after they climbed over the wall, their disappearance was discovered. Prison guards soon followed in hot pursuit with flashlights and police dogs. As the dogs began to gain ground on the convicts, one of the escapees got a bright idea and ran up a tree. The other convict, who had difficulty making decisions, thought he'd better follow suit. He ran up a tree about 50 feet away.

When the dogs reached the first tree, they were in a frenzy, barking and jumping in the direction of the convict. The guards surrounded the tree and began to shine their flashlights upward. The first convict thought fast and said, "Coo-coo, Coo-coo!"

One of the prison guards shouted, "Oh, it's just a dumb bird." Pulling the dogs away, they ran to the next tree. Once again the dogs began to bark loudly. The second convict thought as quickly as he could and chose an animal he felt he could imitate.

"Moo!" he said.

Unfortunately, cows don't live in trees!

It takes a wise man to know his proper role. And it takes a married man of wisdom to grasp the tremendous significance of God's desire and design for his life. He must examine and accept submission to God's Word, to his pastor, to his employer and to the authorities in the land. Contrary to what the world is trying to force us to believe, man has been called to deal with much more than woman with regard to marital responsibilities.

Once I understood what God had called my husband to do in regard to me, I had an urge to run to the local drugstore and buy him a sympathy card. He is to guide and direct me in all my defiance, stubbornness and rebellion. He's responsible for my spiritual condition, even when I'm a real basket case. He is to love me when I am unlovely. He is to live with me in an understanding way, when many times I don't understand myself.

A Dream Come True?

Imagine a husband coming home after a long day's work, pulling into the driveway, and before he can shift the car into park, his smiling wife rushes out to greet him. She is dressed as if she'd just stepped out of *Vogue*. The children are right behind her. One of them carries a cool glass of lemonade. The other has his house slippers. Dad is ushered into the house and taken into the family room where the TV is turned to his favorite show. The children all kiss him, leave to do their homework and are not seen for the rest of the night.

Husband's dinner is placed on a tray, and the TV adjusted for comfortable viewing. Finally when the TV screen turns white, the wife knows it's time for him to retire. She descends in a flowing negligee, leads him to a hot bath, washes his back and then joins him in bed.

Do you think a husband could deal with that? It's certainly a delightful scenario from a man's point of view. And if a woman wishes to treat her husband that way, that's her privilege. But such pampering should never become his goal or expectation. God did not call the Christian husband to *leisure*. He called him to *leadership*. Let's take a look at what Scripture admonishes husbands to do.

The Husband Is the Head

> But I would have you know, that the head of every man is Christ; and the head of the woman is the man; and the head of Christ is God (1 Corinthians 11:3).

Now that seems simple enough. The woman yields to the man, the man to Christ, and Christ to God. So what's the problem? The problem is multifaceted and varies with each marriage. However, we usually find the greatest challenges in these areas:

1. The husband refuses to accept the responsibility of being the head or of submitting to God.
2. The wife refuses to submit to the husband.
3. In-laws or others outside the immediate family unit are allowed to influence the decisions of the family.
4. The flesh—not the spirit—is dominant in the marriage relationship.

There's a saying that if you are leading and no one is following, then you are just taking a walk! God devised a plan to keep absolute harmony in our marriage relationships. However, men and women are attempting to rewrite the rules without ever having played the game God's way.

Being the head of a woman can require bulldog tenacity, along with gentle love and understanding. A man has to be humble enough to listen to the opinions of his wife, yet strong enough to go in the direction he feels God is leading him.

It should be noted that when we stand before the judgment seat of Christ to receive our rewards, the man—not the woman—will have to give an account for the direction he took his family. We clearly see that in the case of Adam and Eve. The Scriptures are so specific that there is no need for a married man to guess at what God has commanded him: "For the husband is the head of the wife, even as Christ is the head of the church" (Ephesians 5:23).

What does it mean for a man to be a Christlike "head" of his wife? It means that he is deeply concerned about her well-being. He is sacrificially committed to every aspect of her personal growth and fulfillment. He is willing to take full responsibility for her protection and guidance, while leaving her the freedom to be herself and fully develop into the unique woman God created her to be. In short, a Christlike husband is dedicated to loving his wife as much as he loves himself.

Christ is the head of the church. He didn't get that position because His Father owned the company; He earned the right. At the time of His earthly life, the Jews thought their Messiah would reveal Himself by defeating their enemies and appearing in majesty. Everyone was unprepared for the carpenter's Son.

> Let this mind be in you, which was also in Christ Jesus; who, being in the form of God, thought it not robbery to be equal with God; but made himself of no reputation, and took upon him the form of a servant, and was made in the likeness of men (Philippians 2:5-7).

Jesus knew who He was. Being secure in the knowledge, He set about to reach everyone. His purpose was to show people everywhere the way to His kingdom. And God's Word exhorts us all to let Jesus' mind be in us.

If a man is going to be the head of his wife as God has instructed, he must first have this mind and be secure in who he is. If he has confessed his sins, openly professed with his mouth the Lord Jesus Christ and believed in his heart that God has raised Him from the dead, he is saved (Romans 10:9). This means that he is a royal priest (1 Peter 2:9) and a joint-heir to the throne of Christ (Romans 8:17).

Being confident with such an impressive spiritual birthright, a husband is able to love his wife without needing to seek a reputation for himself. Like the president of a company, he will want to be actively involved in daily living, assuring himself that nothing transpires within his family that he doesn't know about and approve of. He will be glad to include himself in every facet of family life. In doing so, he willingly takes on the role of a servant.

> For even the Son of Man did not come to
> be served, but to serve, and to give His life a
> ransom for many (Mark 10:45 NASB).

Now men, before you throw this book down in despair, take a look at an excerpt from Charles Swindoll's book *Improving Your Serve*.

> When people follow leaders with a servant's heart, the Lord is exalted....Let me suggest a couple of revealing tests of humility:
>
> (1) A non-defensive spirit when confronted. This reveals a willingness to be accountable. Genuine humility operates on a rather simple philosophy. Nothing to prove. Nothing to lose.
>
> (2) An authentic desire to help others. I'm referring to a sensitive, spontaneous awareness of needs. A true servant stays in touch with

struggles others experience. There is the
humility of mind that continually looks for
ways to serve and to give.[1]

Before my husband matured in the Lord and before I
discarded my confrontational attitude, almost everything
I said to him was responded to defensively. Now that he's
chosen to take on the form of a servant in our relationship, he welcomes my comments. His defenses are down.
And since I know that I don't have to plow through a
seven-foot wall to reach him, I sometimes even find myself
overly concerned with how I express something to him. I
don't want to misuse my freedom nor bruise him.

This clearly applies to marriage relationships. When a
wife can openly share her heart without fear of retaliation
from her husband, she is able to vent her opinions, fears,
and frustrations. Once she knows that her husband has
"heard" her, she can assume that he will integrate her
input into his decision. But in the final analysis, the man
must go in the direction God is leading him whether his
wife agrees or not!

The godly husband is humble enough to listen and
strong enough to lead. Sounds like Jesus, doesn't it?

Husbands, Love Your Wives

Husbands, love your wives, even as Christ
also loved the church, and gave himself for
it (Ephesians 5:25).

What a powerful correlation between a husband's
love for his wife and Christ's love for the church! God

---

1. Charles Swindoll, *Improving Your Serve* (Waco, TX: Word, Inc.,
   1981).

could have used examples of human men who loved their wives dearly such as Hosea or Elkanah. But He wanted to identify marital love with something much deeper and grander.

How much did Christ love the church? He died and gave Himself for it. He sacrificed His life that the church might live. And He did so in spite of the fact that He knew the church would not always meet His expectations. The Lord's plans were long-range. So ought a husband's plans be for his wife.

A husband should be as concerned about his wife's future as he is about his own. How is her health—physically, mentally, spiritually? What are her gifts? How are they being developed? What are her dreams? What is she looking forward to? When the children are grown, what will she do with her time? When he retires, will her life be as rewarding as his? If he were to die, how would she support herself? If she were to die, would she be looking forward to her heavenly home?

Most women would be deeply gratified to know that their husbands were genuinely concerned with these issues in a caring, nonmanipulative way. And when the bonds of marriage are strengthened by such foresight and kindness, a woman's role of submission takes on a new and unthreatening perspective. Why not submit to a prayerful husband who has your best interests at heart?

One day a man overcome with emotion entered the office of my pastor, Dr. E.V. Hill, and tearfully explained the difficulties he was having with his wife. After the man went through a long list of faults, my pastor asked him, "What was she like when you married her?"

"Oh, pastor," he quickly replied, "she wasn't anything like she is today. She was so nice."

My wise pastor responded, "Well, she became the way she is now under your leadership!"

I once heard Frank describe his love for me as we ate dinner with a friend. He said, "Sometimes I love Bunny as my wife. Other times I love her as my friend. But there are instances when I don't feel love for her as a wife or a friend. Then I love her as my sister." God's unconditional agape love always finds a way to express itself to others.

Christ showed His love for the church by humbling Himself and setting an example. He didn't tell the disciples to wash each other's feet; He showed them. Some women do not know how to submit because they do not know what submission looks like. Perhaps they were raised in a female-dominated family. Perhaps other situations occurred that did not provide a proper role model for them.

Christian marriage starts off on the right foot when the wife comes into the marriage with the understanding of God's pattern for marital submission and intends to operate according to His established order. However, if she doesn't, it is the husband's responsibility to exemplify submission for her.

How? I mentioned in the first chapter that my husband's humility and kindness drew me to him. Although those are great attributes, it does not mean he understood how God wanted him to lead me and his family. Nevertheless, I learned submission by watching my husband.

Frank was raised by his father and mother in a family of five. His father was a man of few words—either to his wife or to his children. Frank—the middle child—never once heard his father say "I love you."

When God's Word challenged Frank to love me as Christ loved the church, he had few human role models to emulate. But because of his love for God, I watched him, little by little, break through the negative patterns of his past.

For the first few years of our marriage, almost every time I shared ideas or opinions, Frank simply said, "That's dumb!"

This hurt me deeply. I felt insulted and rejected. I'd react with, "That's *not* dumb. That's just the way I think."

"Ninety-five percent of the people in the world," he would reply, "agree with me and five percent agree with you. I still say that's dumb!"

As Frank grew closer to the Lord and began to submit to God's loving leadership, he changed his communication style. He humbled himself to listen and consider, even when he didn't agree. Now he tells his children daily how much he loves them and demonstrates his love for me in many different ways. He has staunchly refused to allow his past to "press him into a mold." Instead, he has been "transformed by the renewing of his mind."

The Husband Is the Spiritual Leader

Frank's "renewed mind" has allowed him to set a spiritual example for me and the girls in our home. I have been observing him for years, and his obedience to God has provided me with the godly leadership I need.

A few years ago, Frank was about to make a specific business decision. The transaction would have brought a lot of money to us, but would have shortchanged another person. As we were sharing in Proverbs one day, he read, "A false balance is abomination to the Lord, but a just weight is his delight" (Proverbs 11:1).

Rather than attempting to justify the more profitable arrangement, Frank changed directions and actually was more than fair to the other person. I was watching!

Sometimes Frank would disagree with decisions our pastor made. He would share his thoughts with him, in love, and then follow our pastor's decision without murmuring or grumbling. I was watching!

Even though driving down the freeway at 70 mph is more Frank's style, he learned to humble himself to the authorities of the land. He has reduced his speed to the limit. I was watching!

> Now therefore fear the Lord, and serve him in sincerity and in truth....And if it seem evil unto you to serve the Lord, choose you this day whom ye will serve; whether the gods which your fathers served that were on the other side of the flood, or the gods of the Amorites, in whose lands ye dwell; but as for me and my house, we will serve the Lord (Joshua 24:14,15).

Joshua said, "As for me and my house, we will serve the Lord." Being the spiritual leader of the wife can be a most difficult challenge. Satan often meets the one who bears this responsibility head-on, and the gates of hell will stand defiantly before him. Still, there is no mistaking God's direction for husbands in this vital area.

My husband and I teach a quarterly marriage enrichment class. One of the couples' assignments is to rearrange their schedules so they have five to ten minutes of spiritual devotions daily. All we ask is that they read one chapter of Proverbs each day and pray together. We explain that the wife may initiate it, but if it's not being done, the husband is responsible. When we meet at the end of the week, we ask each couple to give a report of how many times they shared a devotional time. Guess what? The answer is usually once or twice, at the most.

Why is there such a resistance to devotion and prayer on the husband's part? For one thing, men sometimes don't want to allow their wives to see their frailties exposed by the Word. But it seems to me that Satan is the one offering the most resistance. He *knows* the power of prayer. And remember what was shared in Chapter 3? We discovered that leadership is foreign territory to men. And it's never so clearly seen as in this spiritual area.

The Bible says God has given us immense power when two or more people agree in prayer. We married couples are potential spiritual dynamos! Yet husbands and wives pass each other daily and never take advantage of what God has placed in their own homes. Just think what would happen in this world if all the Christian spouses came together before the Lord, asking Him to make them lights in the world. If only we could catch the vision!

Husbands must learn to pull down Satan's strongholds in this area.

They should lead their wives in devotion and prayer on a daily basis.

Living Together According to Knowledge

> Likewise, ye husbands, dwell with them according to understanding [knowledge], giving honour unto the wife, as unto the weaker vessel, and as being heirs together of the grace of life; that your prayers not be hindered (1 Peter 3:7).

I'm sure if you're a husband, you've already noticed that your wife thinks quite differently than you. God designed woman specifically as a helpmeet—to help complete that side of man that is incomplete without her. (More about this later!) However, if a man does not take the time to study the uniqueness God has placed in her to help him, he will definitely come up short in the matter of understanding. Husbands have to be careful *not* to think like the writer of the following poem:

> Believe as I believe, no more, no less
> That I am right, and no one else, confess
> Feel as I feel, think as I think
> Eat what I eat, and drink what I drink
> Look as I look, do always as I do
> And then, and only then, I'll fellowship
> with you.
>
> —Anonymous

Husbands should ask themselves one very relevant question: "If your wife were a required subject at a local university, would you pass the course?"

One pastor's wife shared with me her personal frustration. So often she'd watched her husband encourage and respond favorably to other women in the church. Yet he was critical and inattentive to her. It wasn't that she suspected he was overly involved with the other women. He simply made her feel completely insignificant. Many men refuse to submit to God's Word and invest time in getting to know their wives. Even fewer men know how to communicate with them.

I remember hearing about "John and Betty," attending their first couples' conference, where there was a strong emphasis on affection and intimacy. John felt uncomfortable watching the warm interaction between many of the couples. Nevertheless, he thought if he pretended well enough, his inhibitions wouldn't be discovered.

During lunch he chose a table with two other couples who had been to several conferences. The two husbands seemed to have it all together. After their plates had been placed before them, the husband on his right looked into his wife's eyes and said, "Pass the sugar, Sugar."

The second husband spoke tenderly to his spouse, "Pass the honey, Honey."

John thought quickly and said, "Pass the tea, Bag!"

Husbands may have some uncomfortable moments ahead before they actually begin to relate lovingly to their wives or to communicate with them. But when men begin to unwrap the wifely gifts they've been given, I think they'll be amazed at what God has placed inside the package.

And by the way, men, how's your prayer life? Interestingly, the last part of God's exhortation to husbands says that their prayers will be hindered if this kind of personal knowledge is not pursued. Feelings of resentment growing from selfish conduct in the home will render effective prayer difficult—prayer which must be offered "without wrath."

Well, suffice it to say that husbands have quite a load to carry! But oh, how brightly the light shines when a couple's "oneness becomes a witness." It doesn't always come easily. It's a matter of gradual growth. But consider Paul's beautiful exhortation:

> Brethren, I count not myself to have apprehended; but this one thing I do, forgetting those things which are behind, and reaching forth unto those things which are before, I press toward the mark for the prize of the high calling of God in Christ Jesus (Philippians 3:13,14).

Chapter 5

What Men
Want to Know

〜

Q.

My wife complains that I am not taking the lead in decision making. But when I try, she does everything in her power to usurp my authority. What should I do?

A.

There could be several reasons for this action. First, she may have developed this mode of operation due to your lack of initiative in providing leadership. Or, she may be reacting more out of a habit than in conscious rebellion.

Another possible explanation for your wife's behavior is found in the creation narrative. When God confronts and judges Eve's actions (refer to Chapter 2), Genesis 3:16 explains that a woman's desire will constantly be to control or influence her husband.

A friend of Chinese descent once told me, "My mother was the most submissive woman you could ever meet. She followed all the customs of our country as dealt with husband and wife. But every evening when my parents came home, behind the closed doors I'd watch her yank my father's chain! She ran our house!"

So what can a husband do? We find the answer in Ephesians 6:13,14: "And having done all, to stand." *Stand.*

I suggest you choose an appropriate time, create an atmosphere conducive to positive communication and remind her of your complaint. In short, stand up and be heard!

If she has been taking the leadership in decision making for quite some time, be prepared for her gradual release. You'll need to be patient! How long it will take depends on your obedience to God in taking the authoritative role in your home. You may not win any popularity contests, but you will eventually earn her respect. Ultimately, there will be peace in your home.

It took several years for Frank to impress upon me his God-given right to make the final decisions. But I thank God for every day that he stood his ground.

It has been said that man has a strong desire to go out, slay the dragon and bring it home to his wife. Unfortunately, many men have discovered the dragon is not outside the home...she's within it!

Q.

When I try to explain to my wife my rationale for making a decision that she doesn't agree with, she becomes emotional and starts to cry. I don't want to give in, but I can't bear to see her cry!

A.

The emotional side of a woman brings a balance to the logical side of man. When a woman feels strongly about an issue and is put into a position where she cannot exercise her judgment, an emotional response is normal. Give your wife freedom to express her emotions. But don't allow her tears to influence your decision. Always remember that it will be you—not your wife—who will answer to God for the direction in which you took your family. Therefore, listen to her opinions on the issue (that means looking at her when she's talking and not cutting her off), and when she is finished, consider her points. Then make your decision.

Should you make the wrong decision, be sure

you acknowledge it. However, never give up your God-given right to lead.

Q.

My wife and I have an ongoing battle about her working. I feel that raising our children and taking care of the home is a full-time job. She says that I'm just trying to suppress her talents. What should I do?

A.

You're right when you say that raising children and taking care of your home is a full-time job. As a matter of fact, I always refer to it as an alternative career. It takes all the dedication of a woman going for her master's degree. It involves delayed gratification and receiving little appreciation. However, when it comes to intangibles, I believe that being a full-time mother is possibly the most highly-paid profession a woman can pursue!

The money earned while working outside the home is often spent quickly. It can't be taken with us when we leave this earth. On the contrary, a mother affects up to four generations of offspring, and the investment that she makes in the lives of her children continues long after she is gone. Who can better instill the proper character, integrity, responsibility and discipline into the lives of her children?

On the other hand, I understand your wife's frustration about not being able to fulfill her potential in a productive manner. I suggest that the two of you discuss some alternatives for allowing her to operate a business out of her home. Many a millionaire has emerged from a home business.

I operate a network marketing business out of my home which I find profitable and fulfilling. It gives me the opportunity to exercise my talents, yet I can control my schedule so I'm available to my husband and children.

Actually, one can save quite a bit of money by operating a business at home. There are legitimate tax deductions available. And a home business also eliminates the need for babysitters, along with other additional costs such as wardrobe, lunches and transportation.

I suggest you show a genuine interest in your wife's need to express her talents. I think you'll be surprised at what develops!

I know that I'm supposed to be the man of the house, but I often feel like the "mouse of the house." My wife belittles me in front of the children and frequently disagrees with me in their presence. I find myself becoming more and more withdrawn. What do you suggest?

A.

You may have heard the expression that "most men have a wishbone instead of a backbone." They can only wish their wives would submit to their authority and respect and admire them.

However, a great majority of women haven't come from an environment where that kind of an example was set. Sadly, your own children are observing your family's behavior now, and they, too, will begin to incorporate it into their own lives once they are married.

First, a husband needs to realize what awesome responsibilities he has in setting an example for his children. He makes it possible for them to eventually live productive and balanced lives.

Second, he must acknowledge that he cannot do it by himself, but needs the direction and guidance of God's Word, his pastor and his personal relationship with Jesus Christ.

The Lord can strengthen you to be the kind of husband He created you to be. Through God's Word you will learn to be a leader—not a dictator: to rule with a hand of steel that is covered with velvet, and to love your wife as Christ loved the church and gave Himself up for it.

If your wife loves the Lord and His Word, she will eventually accept her rightful position in your relationship. If she does not know the Lord, then it is your responsibility to firmly, yet lovingly, reflect Christ so that she will be drawn to Him. A decision must be made by you to submit to God's Word and take the position of leadership in your home. It won't be easy, but you will have the Lord on your side.

Q.

My wife is a lovely person, but a terrible housekeeper! My pleas have gone unheeded. I find it very difficult to respond to her in a positive way because I believe that if she loved me, she would extend herself in this area which is important to me. What can I do?

A.

I met a woman once who shared with me that she was a terrible housekeeper and was divorced from her first husband because of it. She said if she had to clean house, she just wouldn't get married. That fascinated me. When I inquired as to why she felt so strongly about the issue, she began to share her life's story with me.

I discovered that she grew up with a mother who never allowed her to help with the housework. She was continuously told she was inadequate and would do it wrong if she tried. Her one and only attempt turned out to be a disaster.

Soon after she was married, her husband went to work and she was determined to clean the kitchen floor.

"The kitchen floor looked like Grand Central Station," she told me, "and I had no idea where to begin. I sat in the middle of the floor and broke out into a cold sweat." The woman's fear of failure was so overwhelming that it paralyzed her. When her husband came home, he was furious and accused her of being lazy and worthless. One thing led to another, and the end result was a divorce.

Most of the time, a woman who is a terrible housekeeper is either the product of an environment that was overly clean or totally unclean. In either case, she is unbalanced in her thinking as to the importance of a clean home. She probably feels the task is extremely arduous and taxing. One thing is certain: too much pressure can have negative results and will place undue strain on the relationship.

Start by carefully listening to your wife's description of a clean house. Let her tell you what she feels her responsibility is in the upkeep of the home. Ask questions that will allow her to freely share her concerns and apprehensions.

Once you've heard her out, ask God to give you directions as to how you can constructively help her turn the ordeal into an ideal situation. There are so many things that can be done to make housework enjoyable, and maybe even fun!

Don't fall into the trap of thinking that just because she's a woman she should know how to clean. Develop ideas that will help build her self-esteem and encourage her in that area.

If you can afford it, you may want to consider hiring a cleaning person on a weekly basis.

Whatever you do, your wife will appreciate your understanding, as well as your commitment to your home and relationship.

The Bible says to "live with your wife in an understanding way." No two women are alike, so make sure you don't compare her with anyone. In time, she will grow stronger in that area.

Who knows? Maybe then she can turn her attention to one of *your* weaknesses!

Q.

I work hard to provide for my family, but I'm finding it impossible to keep up with my wife's spending habits. I am experiencing a great deal of stress and she doesn't seem to understand what effect this is having on our relationship. I need your help.

A.

In our society, it is difficult to live within our means. You can hardly enter a store without someone offering you a credit card with a 90-day delayed payment. Meanwhile, television, magazines and billboards remind us of how inferior we are unless we're able to meet the visual standards set up by advertisers and Hollywood. Peer pressure is on adults and children alike to dress well, wear the latest hairstyles and makeup, and drive the "right" cars. As the head of your home, ask yourself some of these questions:

1. Who are your wife's friends and what are their lifestyles?

2. Are your neighbors continuously buying something new to show off to the neighborhood?

3. What type of schools do your children attend? Does the fashion consciousness there demand that they keep up?

4. When does your wife spend the most money: when she's happy, depressed, worried, tired, etc.?

5. Does your wife feel fulfilled with your love?

6. Do you give her quality time and attention?

These questions will begin to give you some clues about the actions of your wife, and can help you open up new areas of communication and understanding. Many times, shopping is a replacement for a void in our lives. Or, if peer pressure is the motive, you may want to consider a possible change in environment. Even some churches put a tremendous emphasis on a person's financial status and appearance.

Your wife is sending out a strong message. If you're currently tuned to one channel, let me suggest that you tune to another quickly. You'd better get on her frequency!

Q.

It's my understanding that once we're married,

it displeases God when we do not submit our bodies to one another. My wife and I are both Christians, but it seems that the concept was never accepted by her. I don't want to go outside our home to be fulfilled sexually, but she constantly denies me. What should I do?

A.

If you're a Christian, then you know that going outside of your home to be sexually fulfilled is not an option. You married your wife for better or worse, and it appears that you are currently dealing with the worst. A woman may deny her husband sex for several reasons: a distorted childhood, a lack of intimacy in their relationship, a perverted concept of what sex is, physical problems or mental and emotional inhibitions.

Those possibilities just scratch the surface of an area where Satan has attempted to rule supreme. Each case is individual, and I would suggest that the two of you consider quality counseling. Many books have been written on the subject of sex that might assist you in this challenge. If your wife was special enough to marry, then she's special enough to receive the benefit of your love, concern and understanding.

Don't let this difficult situation diminish the tremendous capabilities you have to be a happy and satisfied couple. Invest in your wife with time and counseling. I feel sure your returns will prove to be worth it.

Q.

Every now and then when my wife and I do not agree, she says to me, "I think you should submit to me on this matter because I submitted to you the last time. The Bible says in Ephesians 5:21 'Submitting yourselves one to another in the fear of God.'" What should I say?

A.

I am relieved to hear that I am not the only wife who's tried to use Ephesians 5:21 as a method of getting her own way. I remember the first time I used that Scripture on my husband; it sent him scrambling to the Word for an answer. What he discovered puts an end to your dilemma.

Let's take a look at the Scripture to which your wife is referring and to the Scripture that follows:

> Submitting yourselves one to another in the fear of God. Wives, submit yourselves unto your own husbands, as unto the Lord (Ephesians 5:21,22).

The first thing you must realize is that the word "submit" does not mean the same thing in both verses.

If you start reading Ephesians 5 from verse 1, you'll eventually see that verse 21 concludes a discussion about bringing our lives under subjection to God through Christian conduct.

In verse 21 the word "submitting" *(hupo-deiknumi)* means "to exhibit under the eyes of, to exemplify or show."

In verse 22 the word "submit" *(hupotasso)* means "to place in an orderly fashion under." This word demonstrates one's relation to superiors, through compulsory or voluntary subordination.

Submission in a marriage relationship does not work in exactly the same way as does mutual submission in the body of Christ. In the body of Christ we submit to one another by practicing scriptural principles. In marriage, we submit to the husband as an authority figure.

In Ephesians 5:21, the only authority in view is God.

In Ephesians 5:22, the wife is placed in submission to her husband. God gives the husband authority over the wife, and He also holds him accountable.

So what should you say to your wife when she wants you to submit to her decision? Try this:

"Honey, please pray with me! With God's help I'll make the right choice for both of us, and He will be pleased. Because, you know, I'm really the one who's going to have to answer to the Lord someday for all our family's decisions."

Chapter 6

Submission and the Married Woman

⌐∽

The submissive married woman is a woman of faith, strength, and power! No, that is not a contradiction, but an amazing paradox. We are liberated by the very principle that Satan has worked so hard to distort: submission.

What are we liberated from? First, we are free from an "image" or "identity" that suggests we are inferior and subservient. Second, we are released from a prison whose bars represent rebellion, defensiveness, contempt and frustration. That prison's guards are unbelief and its walls are fear. And there is but one key that will unlock the doors: the key of faith.

> But without faith it is impossible to please
> him; for he that cometh to God must believe
> that he is, and that he is a rewarder of them
> that diligently seek him (Hebrews 11:6).

Women of Faith

It takes a woman of faith to believe that God *is,* God *knows* and God *will.*

Many Christian married women who have difficulty comprehending God's plan for submission assume that the Christian Scriptures cannot be taken literally. They have concluded that when you consider the time period in which the Bible was written (2,000 years ago), and who wrote the books (men), you come up with a one-sided, biased and distorted view of God's intentions.

But that perspective is unacceptable to those of us who know that the Bible is God's Word, and that all Scripture is "God-breathed." Also, we cannot help but notice that the principle of submission runs consistently from the first page of the Bible to the last. And as we've seen before, submission applies to everyone!

There are few areas in life that Satan has not attempted to pervert, but submission to authority has always been high on his list of priorities. For one thing, rebellion against God's authority is what caused him to be cast out of heaven. For another, he realizes the power contained in the submission principle can be devastating to his evil agenda.

Satan's Best Tactic

Let's imagine for a moment that you've been given the task of distorting the principle of submission in the hearts and lives of God's children. What approach would you take? I've given this a great deal of thought, and I'm pretty sure I would do exactly what Satan does!

First, I would isolate one group of people: married women. Then I would begin to point out through various means and media the gross "injustice of God." I'd make submission seem ridiculous: How could God make such intelligent, stimulating and accomplished creatures subservient and inferior to their husbands?

At the same time, husbands would be given a "macho" image. They would be influenced to listen to no other advice except their own. On another front, free-spirited single people would be applauded for being independent, with no one to please but themselves.

What a marvelous scheme! Not only is it marvelous, it's working.

While Satan dances around sprinkling anti-submissive dust on God's children, many of us have been rendered powerless against his devices. We not only refuse to surrender to God's Word in this area of our lives, we also produce a list of justifications to cover every situation. The amazing part of all this is that Satan has led us to believe that being independent is *our* idea.

It seems that at some point, in some generation, we ought to catch on to his game.

Why is submission so dangerous to Satan? Why is it so powerful? Because we exercise it in blind faith, and faith defeats him every time.

When we go against our feelings, thoughts and opinions and "yield pleasantly" to authority (i.e., our Lord, God's Word, our husband, pastor or employer), and when we turn the results over to God, we step out in faith. We are making a statement that we believe God knows every detail of our circumstances and that He cares. We are avowing that He is a just God, and that by being obedient to His will, we enable Him to handle all obstacles. Now that takes faith!

Does biblical submission mean we don't express how we feel? No. It means we do! It means when there is a difference of opinion with someone in authority, we share how we feel with due respect and love. Then, if the other person continues to disagree, we turn the whole issue over to God in faith. Submission gives God space to show us who is right. The result is peace and harmony in the relationship until such time as God decides to rectify it.

One of the reasons submission is so difficult for women is because we live in a man's world. We can do the same job and get paid less money. We can be more qualified and not get promoted. There is no doubt that men are usually physically stronger. Because of these factors, many women have learned to get their way through manipulation.

Some of us have become "trained manipulators." We know what to say, when to say it and how to say it in order to achieve our ultimate end. The very thought of releasing our subtle controls shatters our logic, reason and rationale. That's why it takes a woman with faith in God to understand that at the foundation of submission lies the very power of God.

Just Plain Rebellious

When the Lord first revealed what I'm sharing with you, it really made a lot of sense to me. I only had one obstacle: a wall of rebellion so thick it made Fort Knox look like a movie prop.

It's been a long time now, but I still remember standing at my kitchen sink thinking about Frank and the argument we'd just had. I hadn't agreed with his decision, and anger was beginning to burn. I can't even remember the details (had I known I was going to write a book, I would have!). But at that moment, I decided to try God's principle of submission.

I whispered a prayer and said, "Lord, I think Frank's wrong, but I will yield pleasantly to his decision and trust (have faith) in You to work it out." Immediately my anger was gone and replaced by anticipation as to how God was going to resolve the situation. There was peace in my heart and in my home. God resolved the problem so speedily I was dumbfounded. No muss. No fuss. Just God!

In that particular early instance, God was especially kind. He doesn't always answer as quickly nowadays. The encouragement I needed then has been replaced by experience, and years of experience have strengthened my faith. To my amazement, my patience has been developed to such a point that I have no doubt that sooner or later He will resolve any issue we face.

I must admit, by the way, that many times Frank *is* right. And I guess that's understandable. Why would God put a man in a position to be the head of his family if He wasn't planning to give him the wisdom to be a successful leader?

Our greatest challenge with submission is patience. If we can't see something happening "now," we think the problem has gone unnoticed. That's when we are inclined to take things back into our own hands. Unfortunately, this can set the solution back months, and sometimes even years. It's important to remember that "God makes everything beautiful in *His* time."

What If He Makes a Mistake?

During a radio broadcast that featured the topic of submission, the host of the show opened the phone lines for questions. Although I had been given time to explain the principle of submission as it applies to everyone, male or female, as usual all the call-in questions concerned married women. One of the calls was from a gentleman named Jim. He wanted my opinion about a situation involving David, his friend.

David had wanted to make a financial investment. He'd talked it over with his wife and she'd advised him not to do it. David then went to Jim and a few other Christian brothers for suggestions and they had thought the investment was solid. He therefore overruled his wife's advice and made the investment.

The wives of the men who counseled David were very disturbed. They felt it was unfair for him to make that kind of move without his wife's agreement. Their statement was, "She had no choice." Worst of all, it turned out that it was a bad investment. David lost the invested money!

You can imagine what a hot item of debate that became. To even consider the fact that David had the right to make a major investment on his own goes against our fleshly intellect and emotions. And yet, there is no getting around God's Word which says,

> Wives, be submissive to your own husbands *so that even if any of them are disobedient to the word*, they may be won without a word by the behavior of their wives (1 Peter 3:1 NASB).

My response to Jim was that the statement "She had no choice" was incorrect. When David decided to invest, his wife had the choice to submit or rebel. She chose to rebel. Unfortunately, she did not understand the power that is contained in the principle of submission. If the wives who were upset had joined her in intercessory prayer, they would have witnessed the hand of God in that situation.

Does that mean David wouldn't have lost his investment? Perhaps so, perhaps not. Many of us learn by our mistakes. But whatever David needed to learn in this situation *could have* been accomplished through God's intervention in answer to his wife's prayers. And he could have come out of it a much stronger man—not weaker and beaten down.

The key question is, Do you have the faith to believe

that even if your husband makes a mistake, God can make it right?

I used an example that deals with money because it is such a sore spot in our marriages. Countless arguments flare up over the lack of money or how the money we have should be used. We wives need to come to grips with the fact that our husbands are *not* our providers. God is our Provider. The husband is God's choice for head of the home and He will provide through him for the family. And even though we have a tendency to panic when our security is threatened, God is fully equipped to meet our needs, many times through unexpected means.

His Mistake, Her Blessing

The Old Testament Book of Ruth demonstrates one of the countless ways God can rectify a situation after a woman submits to her husband's decisions. In chapter 1 we read that there was a famine in Bethlehem. Elimelech decided to move his wife, Naomi, and two sons to Moab, a heathen nation. God had sent the famine because of Israel's sin. But Elimelech had chosen to run from the chastening of God and to seek relief in a heathen land— clearly a foolish decision.

Naomi was in Moab for ten years. After her two sons married Moabite women, both they and Elimelech died. When heartsick Naomi heard that God was once again blessing Israel, she decided to return to Bethlehem. Ruth, one of her daughters-in-law, clung to Naomi and pleaded to go with her. Ruth finally succeeded in convincing her mother-in-law that she wanted Naomi's people to be her people and Naomi's God to be her God.

Once in Bethlehem, Ruth went to the barley fields to glean food for herself and her mother-in-law. Through her diligence and faithfulness, she came to the attention of Boaz, a wealthy kinsman of Naomi's. Eventually, Boaz married Ruth.

In obedience to her husband's bad decision, Naomi had left her happy home for Moab, only to return to Bethlehem a destitute widow with no surviving children or grandchildren. But now she was wealthy—wealthier than before, and Ruth's first son became hers because of Jewish law. Naomi was provided for all the rest of her life, and had a grandson to carry on the family name. That son was Obed, father of Jesse, who was the father of Israel's mighty king, David. Jesus Himself was born out of the lineage of Naomi.

Does this suggest that God will kill your husband if he makes a mistake? No! But it does reveal how God takes care of us when we remain under the authority of God's established order. Naomi's relief did not come instantly, but it eventually happened. We must remember to give God time—lots of time—to work things out in our lives.

Earlier, I explained how Frank and I surrendered ourselves to the Lord a year after we were married. Shortly thereafter, his music producer's contract ran out and it was necessary to sign again. At that time, Frank was a tremendous success and record companies were clamoring after him with contracts. However, he decided that his relationship with the Lord was of greater importance to him, and that he would not sign with anyone until he was sure about where God wanted him.

Without a producer's agreement, our income dropped

dramatically and immediately, and we soon found ourselves in dire financial straits. Nevertheless, God intervened and provided for us. We started having Bible studies at our home twice a month with an average of a hundred in attendance. As I look back now, I do so with great rejoicing. Frank was right to wait on God. A record deal would have locked him into a contract for years, and his service to God would have been hindered.

I had made my own commitment to God that I never wanted my praise for Him to diminish, no matter what. And I can truly say that although every day was a walk of faith, God always gave me plenty for which to praise Him.

Frank acknowledges that there have been times when he has made financial mistakes. However, I have decided to do for Frank what Jesus has done for me. When Jesus died, He essentially gave us a checkbook of forgiveness. God's Word says

> If we confess our sins, he is faithful and
> just to forgive us our sins, and to cleanse us
> from all unrighteousness (1 John 1:9).

No matter what the challenge in my marriage, I have given that checkbook of forgiveness to my husband. When Jesus was asked how many times we should forgive a person, He responded "seven times seventy times a day." If Frank makes a mistake, I forgive him. If he were to make the same mistake again, the forgiveness would still be waiting for him. Jesus does that same thing for us every day of our lives.

Exercising forgiveness with each other has helped

accomplish something remarkable in our relationship. It has truly made us "one":

> Therefore shall a man leave his father and his mother, and shall cleave unto his wife; and they shall be one flesh (Genesis 2:24).

Allowing each other to make mistakes releases us from condemnation. He knows that I am pulling for him, and if something goes wrong, I believe by faith that God will work it out. Frank has become my best friend—really a part of myself. Whenever a mistake is made and he sees that I was right, he becomes more attentive to my opinions. Communication is open and flowing. We continue to grow together.

The question was "What if my husband makes a mistake?" The answer is "He *will* make mistakes because he is human." The second question is "Are you willing to exercise your faith and believe that whatever the mistake is, God can fix it?" I hope your answer is *"Yes!"*

The Trouble with Eve

Speaking of mistakes, Eve got into trouble when she stood before the tree of knowledge of good and evil and wondered what it might be like to be just like God. That's what caused her to open herself up to Satan's incredible suggestion. Why didn't God punish Eve so she'd never wonder again? Because wondering wasn't the sin. The sin was her choice to be independent and disobey God.

If I were to spend my time wondering how I could serve and love God better, that would be constructive wonderment. If I use that same ability to wonder about being "equal" with God or "playing God" in my circumstances, I will have destroyed the very reason God created me: for His good pleasure.

A woman's need to satisfy her insatiable curiosities was inherited from Eve. I am always amazed at the things that concern me that don't even enter my husband's mind. We meet a lot of women in our marriage counseling classes, and I have found most of them to be curious creatures, too.

God uses submission to channel our curiosity, to make it subject to Himself. It appears to me that submission to our husbands is the insulation God has provided within marriage to protect us from repeating Eve's mistake. I suspect that God assigned women the task of submitting not because they were *not* strong, but because they were *too* strong. With no authority, a woman might have a tendency to create her own kingdom, void of any dependency on God. This, by the way, is reflected in the lives of many women around us who have disregarded the principle of submission.

On the other hand, in the garden, Adam had the ability to make a righteous decision and take a stand. But he lacked the inner strength to stick to his convictions because of his love for Eve. God is developing a quality of leadership in him by making him head of the house.

All of my children are different. I have to instruct each of them individually with an eye toward their unique character development. I don't expect them to like my correction or to understand it; I just expect them to obey. They cannot always grasp the basis upon which my decisions are made. I realize that most of my guidance won't be appreciated until they are adults and have children of their own.

Maybe one morning we'll wake up and realize God knew what He was doing when He assigned Adam and Eve their roles. He knows something about us that we don't know! And I've personally discovered there is no such thing as compromise or negotiating with God. In order to be happy, fruitful and abundant women of God, we need to seriously accept the fact that He is not going to change His mind.

We *must* obey His Word by faith.

The Just Shall Live by Faith

As a matter of fact, God's spiritual vision for us can be summed up in one word: *faith*. It takes faith to see our husbands as they can be and not as they are. It takes faith to submit when we think they're wrong. It takes faith to wait for God to show us which one of us is right, while having no murmurings or grumblings between us. It takes faith to believe that God can give our husbands the wisdom they need to make decisions that affect us and our children.

In the first psalm, we learn that we should meditate on God's law day and night. Here are a few Scriptures I think about throughout the day:

> Faith is the substance of things hoped for, the evidence of things not seen (Hebrews 11:1).

> And whatsoever ye shall ask in my name,
> that will I do, that the Father may be glorified
> in the Son. If ye shall ask any thing in my
> name, I will do it (John 14:13,14).

And do it He will! I started out believing God for little things. And every time He showed me His faithfulness, my faith would stretch a little further. No doubt David experienced the same results and said, "O taste and see that the Lord is good" (Psalm 34:8).

There is a wonderful effortlessness in submitting. You become very comfortable and relaxed. It provides you with a taste of heaven. No longer do we have to be defensive—God is our defense! There is no reason to rebel when we know that God has everything in control.

We believe that one day we will stand before the judgment seat of Christ. At that time we will not be judged with regard to our salvation, but according to our works. It is quite a relief to realize that when we operate under the covering of those God put in authority, it is them—not us—who will answer for the decisions that have been made.

If you aren't careful, you could actually begin to like submitting!

The Extreme Cases

I do want to bring up a rather tragic subject. Jesus reminded us on more than one occasion that some people have very hard hearts. When the phone lines begin to light up on a radio talk show, one of the first questions

I'm asked is, "What if there is physical abuse involved? Am I to submit?"

My answer is always an emphatic "No!"

I quickly recommend that abused women take their children, leave home and find shelter. This makes it possible for the person mistreating them to get help. Whether it's physical or substance abuse, the loved ones involved often find themselves acting as "enablers," unwittingly supporting the abuser's bad habits in any number of ways. Such participants are called "codependents," and they can actually block an abuser's way to recovery and healing.

I am not suggesting that a woman is to desert a difficult marriage, but she must protect herself and her children. She needs to challenge her spouse to get help by demonstrating tough love. The abuser may not respond immediately. And he may hit an all-time low in his life before turning around. Still, there are thousands of recovering addicts and abusers who testify that their recovery was initiated by firm and unwavering actions taken by their loved ones.

In such cases, Christian counseling needs to be sought. But—please—make sure it's really Christian. Psalm 1:1 exhorts us all, "Blessed is the man that walketh not in the counsel of the ungodly."

Seeking God's face through fasting and prayer, and finding the Bible's perspective for your situation can greatly strengthen you. Don't be afraid to lean on your solid Christian friends. There are also many support groups and agencies which are specifically designed to

inform you and help you through your difficult ordeal.
Perhaps your church can help you locate them.

R & R

I hope with all my heart you are *not* a victim of extreme
circumstances. And I hope you have made the decision to
submit to your husband based on what you have read.
If so, you're probably wondering where to begin. Knowing the mind of a woman, you've begun developing a
strategy that will bring you success in your endeavor.
Let me suggest that you begin with some R & R. In the
physical world that means "rest and relaxation." In the
spiritual world it means "repentance and reverence." In
Ephesians 5:33 we read: "And [let] the wife see that she
reverence her husband."

A woman who demonstrates reverence for her husband
will have no difficulty submitting. In the Greek, "reverence" means to be "in deep awe or respect of." If you're
thinking to yourself, "She doesn't know my husband!"
then you need a more complete understanding of what
it means to have reverence for him.

As I meditated on the word "reverence," I asked God
to give me a relevant example. Not long thereafter, He
showed me a picture of former President Reagan walking
into Congress. As our Chief Executive made his entrance,
everyone rose to his feet in honor of Reagan's lofty position. No one would have denied that there were many
people in that room who were opposed to Reagan's poli-
tics. If it had not been for his position, they would not
have stood. They were honoring his presidency, not his
policies.

On a prestigious television interview show, former Vice President George Bush was being interviewed regarding the Iran contra scandal. Based on the line of questioning, it appeared that the host of the program felt Bush had knowledge of the Iran affair. Several times during the interview the commentator's attitude was brisk and curt. When he was finally out of time, the journalist cut the Vice President off sharply and concluded the program.

The public was outraged! Television executives were embarrassed. Letters began to pour in. Were they angry because they thought Bush was not involved with the scandal? No. People were upset because of the lack of respect shown to a person holding the position of Vice President.

We may not respect our husbands for the type of men they are, for their decisions or their leadership. However, God demands that we respect the position He has placed them in as husbands. I asked the Lord, "Does this mean that I am to stand whenever my husband walks into a room?"

He replied, "No, but your spirit should. Your spirit should stand in honor, and bow in respect. When you vowed to Me that you were accepting him as your husband 'until death do us part,' he became the head of you and your home." God reminded me that this policy is appropriate even in the cases where husbands clearly do not conduct themselves in a respectable manner.

After God had finished unfolding the meaning of reverence, I hung my head and wept. I realized that I had had enough "marriage sense" to be respectful to my husband on the exterior, but I knew in my heart that

I'd never had reverence for him. Rarely did we have a conversation where my inward spirit was not rebelling at Frank's words.

I had never even considered the position that God had placed him in. I repented. I said, "God, I didn't know. From this day forward, I will not be irreverent to my husband; not in words, thoughts or actions. And if I should slip, Father, I will go to him and ask his forgiveness."

From that moment on, my life completely changed. The first thing I noticed was that all the noisy dialogues within me ceased. Have you ever considered the number of conversations you have with your husband inside your head? Many times I would be raging when Frank walked into a room, and he hadn't said a word.

Once I repented, I experienced a peace I would never have thought possible. Today when my husband walks into a room, my spirit stands in honor. It bows in respect to the position he holds. I strive to resist thoughts that would stand against his position. Little did I know that simple obedience to God's Word would open a freedom to me that I had never known.

The benefits of this obedience could not be contained in this book or in hundreds of others. Without my telling Frank about my decision to have reverence for him, he began to change in ways that I never could have imagined in the first 15 years of our marriage. Time after time, I watched him start doing things I had only dreamed might happen. And I began to see my own role as his "helpmeet" clarified.

A Wife, a Helpmeet

> And Adam gave names to all cattle, and to
> the fowl of the air, and to every beast of the
> field; but for Adam there was not found an
> helpmeet for him. And the Lord God...made
> he a woman, and brought her unto the man
> (Genesis 2:20-22).

Are you like me? Up until recently, I thought being a helpmeet meant cleaning the house, taking care of the children and generally keeping things in order. It wasn't until I began reverencing Frank and allowed some growth time to pass that the word "helpmeet" took on a new meaning—the meaning that God originally intended.

The areas in which I had tried to be efficient are certainly necessary to daily living. However, my husband could pay someone to do any one of them. What I am able to offer Frank in our relationship cannot be filled by anyone but me, Bunny—his wife. I bring to him a counterpart to his own personality. When a wife is a true helpmeet, and the two become one, that "one" is complete and whole.

All men and women are deficient in some aspects of their lives. I've come to understand that, as I develop myself spiritually, I become more and more the complement my husband needs to bring positive dimensions to his character and personality. Likewise, Frank's clear-eyed, practical point of view and male perspective balance my more emotional approach to life.

Faith and Freedom

In an effort to be the woman who can best fit that important helpmeet role, I've begun to meditate on God's Word "day and night." Over months and years, I've come to understand more of His truth. And that truth has set me free. I am free to live, free to love, free to discover God's inexplicable riches of wisdom, understanding and knowledge. In obedience to God's Word, my spirit has become gentler and quieter. I have learned to understand 1 Peter 3:1-5:

> Likewise, ye wives, be in subjection to your own husbands; that, if any obey not the word, they also may without the word be won by the conversation of the wives; while they behold your chaste conversation coupled with fear. Whose adorning...let it be the hidden man of the heart, in that which is not corruptible, even the ornament of a meek and quiet spirit, which is in the sight of God of great price. For after this manner in the old time the holy women also, who trusted in God, adorned themselves, being in subjection unto their own husbands.

Why is a wife with a meek and quiet spirit of great price in the sight of God? What makes something of great price? It's rarity! Women who have a meek and quiet spirit and reverence for their husbands are rare indeed. Will you be one of those priceless women of God?

It's important that our vision for our marriage and God's vision be the same. Submission, like love, is an act of our will, and is not only for those who sincerely desire to be obedient children of God. Dare we face Christ at the judgment seat having committed the same offense as Eve? She rebelled against God's beautiful design for her life. The instructions are clear: *wives submit*. We must believe by faith that God knows what He is doing.

> Trust in the Lord with all thine heart; and lean not unto thine own understanding. In all thy ways acknowledge him, and he shall direct thy paths (Proverbs 3:5,6).

I hope if you're ever asked, "Are you a submissive wife?" your answer will be, "Yes, I am a woman of strength and faith and power!"

Then you can smile as your inquisitors walk away with bewilderment written all over their faces!

Chapter 7

What Women
Often Ask

Q.

My husband refuses to take a leadership role
in our home. I want to submit, but he won't make
a decision. What can I do?

A.

Well, there's one decision that we know he
made. He chose to marry you, which means he can

make quality decisions! Perhaps he needs assurance from you that you value his judgments.

When a woman takes over the role or otherwise finds herself being head of her house, she usually adopts certain attitudes toward her husband: one is disdain, the other is disrespect. And neither of those reactions will cause a husband to be a better leader. God created both men and women with egos. If a man's sense of self is properly validated, the encouragement he receives will help him become all he can be. How many times have we heard the saying, "Behind every good man is a good woman"?

If a man has never witnessed leadership in his childhood home, or if that leadership was twisted, he may be shirking his responsibilities due to ignorance or fear. There are several things you can do.

1. It's important to believe Mark 10:27: "With God all things are possible." We must believe that God can do anything, and that includes teaching our husbands to lead.

2. Believe that God will give you the wisdom needed in your particular situation. James 1:5,6 says: "If any of you lack wisdom, let him ask of God, that giveth to all men liberally, and upbraideth not; and it shall be given him."

3. Begin to practice 1 Thessalonians 5:14 (NASB):

"Encourage the fainthearted, help the weak, be patient with all men."

When the Scripture says "all men," that includes your husband! Start looking for things that he does right and begin to give him the praise he deserves. If you administer it three times a day, just like medication, you'll be surprised at his response. Just make sure it's honest praise—not a manipulative ploy.

4. Apply Ephesians 5:33 by faith: "And [let] the wife see that she reverence her husband."

This Scripture teaches us to adore our husbands. Now you may be thinking, "Bunny, you don't know my husband!" It might be hard for you to believe, but the Lord knew all about your husband when He wrote the Scripture. God is all-knowing.

Most husbands have a tendency to come up to our expectations when they honestly believe we look up to them. Let me encourage you to really listen the next time your husband begins discussing any subject. Look at him while he speaks and let him know that you appreciate his communication with you. You'd be surprised at how much your husband will tell you if you'll only listen. But again, be sincere.

5. Make sure you keep your mind where it should be. Isaiah 26:3 says: "Thou wilt keep him in

perfect peace, whose mind is stayed on thee, because he trusteth in thee."

Always remember that you are not, in yourself, able to bring about change. God will, however, use you as His instrument. If you keep your mind focused on Jesus and trust Him to do the changing, you will not become frustrated when it doesn't seem like your husband is changing quickly enough. Never forget that your greatest challenge may not be getting him to take the lead; it may be getting yourself to submit once he does!

Q.

My husband is unsaved—*help!* How can I submit to his decisions when I know he's not being led by God?

A.

Being "unequally yoked" is a painful and challenging matter. There are, of course, disagreements over issues, questions of church attendance and conflicting value systems. But even more tragic is the spiritual warfare that occurs in the home. A heavy, dark oppression can at times overshadow a family in which one spouse does not belong to the Lord.

A Christian married to an unbeliever must seek God's constant companionship, His direction and His covering. Prayerful, supportive friends who can provide biblical counsel are vitally important. And a faith that refuses to judge, preach or in any way manipulate is an absolute necessity.

Even if the husband is not led by God, God still promises to care for His own children. And He has made a solemn commitment to work all things together for good. Being married to an unbeliever is tough, but sometimes the outcome is absolutely miraculous!

Scott, a dear friend of mine in northern California, arrived home one day to find his wife acting differently. He couldn't quite put his finger on it, but they'd been married long enough for him to sense the change. There was a look in her eyes that he had never seen before.

As days went by, Scott noticed that situations and circumstances which would have once caused her to fly off the handle for some reason didn't seem to bother her. Even his favorite saying, which he reserved for use only when he really wanted to make her angry, didn't bring a response. She was loving, yet different. After much contemplating, he finally figured out what had happened: She was having an affair with another man!

All the pieces seemed to fit, and he decided to confirm his suspicions. Since his job was only a 20-minute drive from home, he began making two or three trips home to catch her with her lover. Curiously, she always seemed pleasantly surprised to see him.

After several months, a friend invited them to a social gathering which turned out to be a Christian fellowship. During the evening, an elderly lady approached him and began to share the love of Christ with him. Something about her seemed so familiar. He stared at her intently. Then he saw it! It was her eyes. His wife had the same look in her eyes, and yet she had never mentioned Jesus.

At that moment, Scott knew that his wife had found the Lord. "If Jesus can make this kind of difference in her life," he thought, "I want Him in my life, too!" He gave his heart to the Lord that very night. He is now in full-time ministry and is known nationwide for his love of people and his commitment to Jesus Christ. His wife brought to life 1 Peter 3:1:

> In the same way, you wives, be submissive to your own husbands so that even if any of them are disobedient to the word, they may be won without a word by the behavior of their wives.

Q.

My husband wants to handle the money, but it's because of him that our financial situation is a disaster. I am much more qualified to control this area.

How does submission apply in this instance?

Boy, that's a tough one. The reason it's so difficult to answer is because money is so dear to our hearts. If there is any one thing that keeps a husband and wife from fulfilling God's purpose to become one flesh, it is money, as often as not.

How we handle our finances is just one of the areas that God is concerned about in our lives. The Scriptures speak a lot about money's pitfalls and its power. So in this instance you have to ask yourself, "What is God's desire for my husband in this area?"

Naturally, the answer is that God wants him to be a wise and good steward. So it must be understood first that God is on your side—you and God both want the same thing. However, this is an area that usually takes time and patience on the part of the wife.

We must continually keep in focus our main objective in marriage, which is to become one flesh. Being your husband's helpmeet doesn't necessarily mean you're to take over in his areas of weakness. Instead, it means that you are to believe that God can repair the inadequacies of his life.

I have a personal friend who experienced a situation much like yours. One day her husband decided that he wanted to handle the finances and asked her for the checkbook. In the past, every time he'd done this, their credit had wound up in a shambles. She had already begun to submit to him in other areas and had seen the Lord work miracles in their relationship. It was a tremendous step of faith for her, but she gave him the checkbook.

My friend told her husband she wasn't going to question him about how he spent the money, nor was she going to worry about it. She said she believed God would direct him and that she trusted his judgment. To her surprise, he paid everything on time for two months. Then one day he came in, handed her the checkbook, and told her he was tired of handling it!

This reminds me of a song we sing in our church called "There's Nothing Too Hard for God."

Q.

My husband and I are Christians. We married at a very young age. He pursued his vocation, and I went on to get a college degree. We live in the same house, but we speak different languages. It seems as if he hasn't grown a bit since our wedding day. Any intellectual stimulus I get comes from my job. How can I possibly submit to a man when I don't respect his line of reasoning or his decision-making skills?

A.

Respect is relative. If you're comparing your husband to the suave, worldly wise gentlemen you work with, he'll always come up short. If you compare him with the Word, you'll see that he is a royal priest and joint-heir with Jesus Christ, who owns everything. I'm sure some of the men you work with can't come up to that standard! Paul summed up what he thought about his education (and he was a scholar) in Philippians 3:8: "And I count all things but loss for the excellency of the knowledge of Christ Jesus my Lord."

Being a Christian, your husband also has a jump on many an educated person. Psalm 111:10 says: "The fear of the Lord is the beginning of wisdom."

We must never allow Satan to confuse us concerning worldly "wisdom." We are traveling through a barren land, and this world is not our home. Even though your husband lacks a college education, the Lord is able to bless him so that when he speaks, everybody will listen. You just have to be open to receive it. Also, think of how much you can share with each other if the two of you drop your defenses. Let me encourage you to become fluent in both languages!

Along with these efforts, I would also encourage you to pray for a group of friends with whom you can interact. Whatever your area of interest, during periods of time when your husband is working or busy, God can provide stimulating company that will in no way threaten your marriage.

I am a new Christian and an abused wife. I was also a victim of incest as a child. My husband is unsaved, and I have recently become aware that he stares lustfully at our daughter. I want to stay and believe God, but I'm afraid to stay and afraid to go. How does submission apply in this case?

A.

Your situation is one of those extreme circumstances which needs the guidance of a counselor who understands God's principles and has godly wisdom to make suggestions that could possibly save your children—and maybe even your marriage. It is imperative that you seek good quality Christian counsel, and I strongly suggest you ask your pastor to direct you to someone he trusts. You may have to spend some time away from your husband while the Lord is working on him. A counselor can help you make the best decision.

Q.

My husband is having an affair with another woman and he's not even secretive about it. Am I expected to stay in this situation and submit to his leadership?

A.

I have seen many marriages come to an end because of this devastating sin. Marriage, like our relationship with the Lord, is based on trust.

When that is violated, only agape love (which is unconditional) can keep the relationship together. It is God's desire that we love each other according to 1 Corinthians 13:4-8 (NASB):

> Love is patient, love is kind;...it does not seek its own....[Love] bears all things, believes all things, hopes all things, endures all things. Love never fails.

Sometimes, however, adultery's wounds go very deep, and men and women find it too painful to continue in a broken marriage. God has left room in His Word for those who have been victimized by unfaithfulness.

On the other hand, you may find yourself wanting to hang on to your marriage, praying for eventual repentance on the part of your spouse. If so, it could be that God is giving you faith for a miracle! I recently saw an interview with a couple on a Christian television station. The husband had been blatantly unfaithful for ten years. As a matter of fact, he made it known that he was spending a certain number of days with his mistress and certain other days with his wife.

The wife saw the grip that Satan had on his life, yet she was willing to stand and wait for Jesus to bring the victory. She surrounded herself with fellow Christians who continued to pray for their relationship and for the salvation of her husband. After ten years, he prayed to receive

Christ and he gave up his mistress. Now this couple travels across the country testifying about the power of God, ministering to couples who are facing the same challenge.

Had this wife thrown in the towel, her Christian friends would have understood, and biblically she could have justified her actions. But because of her faith in God, He delivered her and has blessed her abundantly.

When she was asked about whether she ever feels remorse about the years she sacrificed waiting for her husband to change, she replied, "God not only healed my husband, He healed my mind and redeemed the time." Certain people called her a fool, but she believed 1 Corinthians 4:9,10:

> For we are made a spectacle unto
> the world, and to angels, and to men.
> We are fools for Christ's sake, but ye
> are wise in Christ.

Q.

I've tried very hard to be submissive to my husband, but he does so many things to irritate me. Just when I think everything's going well, he'll do something so-o-o dumb! How can I stay on my feet without falling so much?

A.

Learning to submit is like playing the piano. Jesus came and played the composition perfectly to show us it could be done. When we begin to play the same composition, we usually start out with two fingers and work our way up.

There's a song that says, "Yield not to temptation, for yielding is sin. Each victory will help you some other to win." Piano teachers know it will be a while before their students can play well, and because of that they show patience. The Lord knows, too. As for your husband's annoying traits, we all have them. In my marriage I've discovered that the best defense is a good offense.

You can probably make a list of things your husband does that irritate you immensely. I had my own list. And, of course, Frank could list mine. One day I told the Lord I needed Him to show me how I could be delivered from my husband's irritating traits. Let me share a real incident.

Frank used to have a habit of coming into our kitchen while I was in the middle of preparing dinner. He would ask questions that would force me to stop what I was doing and focus my attention on him. This always made me hit the roof. After all, I'm not the best cook anyway (my smoke detector is my dinner bell!), and I try to plan everything to be ready at the same time. Any little thing can throw me off. However, my appeals that Frank not interrupt me went unheeded.

One day after he had left the kitchen, I was hotter than the baked potatoes in the oven. I asked the Lord to forgive my attitude, but told Him I didn't know how to keep from getting angry.

The Lord said, "Now Bunny, since you know he's going to do it anyway, why don't you just accept it?" A light went on in my head and I thought, "Oh, I get it! Just like in football—the best defense is a good offense!" I prayed a short prayer, "Lord, the next time Frank comes into the kitchen while I'm cooking and asks me a question, I'm not going to let it get to me! Lord, give me the strength, and I'll give You the victory."

All at once I was looking forward to Frank's next "interruption."

Each day when I'd start to cook, I would wait for him to arrive at the kitchen door. When he didn't come the first few days, I was actually disappointed! Then, one evening as I was turning the fish over, I heard the familiar sound of him heading my direction. I got so excited I began to smile.

"Lord," I said, "let this challenge result in praise to Your name."

By the time Frank turned the corner to the kitchen, I was almost laughing. Sure enough, oblivious to the fact that I was preparing five courses all at the same time, and with a deep frown on his face he asked, "Bunny, what are these strange numbers on the phone bill?"

I quickly put down the fork I was holding, rushed to his side and, without even a trace of annoyance, simply said, "I don't know, Honey. Let me figure it out and get back with you!" No reaction, no wrath!

As he turned around and left the room, I

saw the ball go over the goalpost, and I heard the crowd roar as a point went up for the home team!

Q.

My husband has never hit me, but he is verbally abusive. Don't you think it's the same thing?

A.

I have been present when husbands and wives verbally abuse one another, and some of the sharpest knives could not compete with the damage of the tongue. However, I do believe verbal and physical abuse are different. Bodily harm endangers your life; verbal abuse is damaging to your emotions and self-image.

So many times a person who is verbally abusive comes from a contemptuous background. Such destructive behavior requires prayerful, serious attention and help. In this case, you may be the help your husband needs. When a person sends out hate and it is met with love, there's no contest. Love is the strongest force on earth:

> Now abide faith, hope, love, these three; but the greatest of these is love (1 Corinthians 13:13 NASB).

When we go against our emotions and will and submit to God's Word, we can trust that God will intervene with a verbally abusive person in

His own time. He will make things right. What is our guarantee? Three little words: "Love never fails."

It is impossible for God's love to fail. Even if the immediate situation defies that Scripture, God's promise is that His love for us *will* never fail. And it always accomplishes that which it set out to do. It is, however, one of the hardest attributes to exercise. God's unconditional love boggles the human mind.

A friend of mine was in a verbally abusive situation for many years. She continued to pray for her husband and to treat him with respect, but she also learned to "disconnect" herself from the unkind words that often assailed her. She did this by focusing her attention on other important matters: her children, her Christian endeavors, her work, her friends and her care of the home. Although wounded and rejected by her spouse, she developed an inner conviction that his words were untrue and unfair and she should not take them to heart. This enabled her to receive God's love and acceptance through the kindness of others.

My friend honestly believed that if she gave the situation to God and trusted Him, He would eventually rectify it. She spent hours in the Word and in prayer. Vital to her survival was a small circle of understanding and encouraging friends who refused to allow her to sink into self-recrimination and depression. Her friends reminded her of "who she was," and encouraged her to be thankful for the positive things in her life.

Finally, a dramatic transformation occurred. After 14 years of cynical and bitter words, the husband was brought face-to-face with his failure. His criticism and insults were silenced within a matter of days. It was my friend's careful and determined obedience to God's voice that finally brought about the change.

God's Word has called us to submit to Him in many areas that are offensive to our mind and flesh. What person in his right mind would want to love his enemies or pray for those who despitefully use him? Yet God calls His children to do just that. Verbal abuse is nothing new to God. His Word equips the believer for handling verbal assaults, with such instructions as "Return blessing for insults" and "A soft answer turns away wrath."

I'm not saying that responding in this way is easy. I'm sure this is one of those instances about which Jesus promises, "They that suffer with me shall reign with me."

To help get you through the pain, I recommend that you surround yourself with a strong group of praying Christians, and that you fortify yourself with God's Word. Learn to see yourself as God sees you. Be sure and read Psalm 139! Once you understand who you are in Him, no one can tear you down.

And look at it this way: Missionaries depart

every day for heathen nations with a mission to take these territories for Christ. You have been given the blessed privilege of being a missionary, and you don't even have to get a passport, pack or leave home!

Q.

For years I have exercised the principle of submission with my husband. I am submissive and reverent, but he appears no closer to the Lord than when I began. His leaving seems imminent, and I don't know what to do.

A.

I once heard a professor of theology say that life in Christ is like a light bulb. The more we surrender to God's will and way, the more transparent we become and the brighter the light grows.

If you have been living a life submitted to God and to your husband, your light is extremely bright. A husband walking in darkness will be continuously bothered by that light. Without you saying a word about Christ, he will be convicted every time he is in your presence. Many times a husband will yield his life to Christ, as we've already discussed.

There are instances, however, when a husband has a hardened heart and refuses to yield to Christ. Your lifestyle, acted out in the power of the Holy Spirit, will either draw him or drive him away. If he decides to leave and you know that you have obeyed God in your conduct toward him (i.e., submitting, reverencing, not denying your body sexually), then 1 Corinthians 7:15 (NASB) would apply to you:

> If the unbelieving one leaves, let him leave; the brother or the sister is not under bondage in such cases.

Some women ask, "How long should I stay in this situation?" Again 1 Corinthians 7:14 (NASB) responds:

> And a woman who has an unbelieving husband, and he consents to live with her, let her not send her husband away.

But, if your husband leaves and you have loved him as the Holy Spirit has called you to love him, you are justified by God's Word to let him go.

If you are concerned about the state of your children, allow 1 Corinthians 7:14 (NASB) to edify and encourage you:

> For the unbelieving husband is sanctified through his wife...otherwise your children are unclean, but now they are holy.

Is it ever right for a woman to disobey her husband?

A.

This is really the ultimate question. In the March/April 1984 edition of *Today's Christian Woman*, some very wise replies were given by two highly respected Christian leaders. This is what they had to say.

Beverly LaHaye: "Before a woman can successfully submit to her husband, she must first submit to Christ. Submitting to the Lord means giving up selfish desires and personal rights. No longer are we alone in our control of our direction and decisions, but the Holy Spirit is to superintend (or govern) our lives.

"Therefore, the only time it is ever right for a woman to disobey her husband is when his direction for her runs in conflict with biblical principles for spirit-filled living. A woman needs, first and foremost, to carefully examine what God's Word instructs her to do. Her top priority should be obedience to her heavenly Father, and then obedience to her husband."

Patricia Gundry: "Of course. It is imperative that Christian wives disobey anyone who tries to usurp God's place in their lives or tries to get them to violate their own consciences.

To do otherwise nullifies the doctrine of the priesthood of the believer and makes Christianity just another religion with another god, rather than a personal relationship between the living God and the individual believer."

I personally believe both statements.

Chapter 8

Submission and the Single Person

Decisions! Decisions! Decisions! Now there's a word that aptly describes the life of the single person. Unattached men and women are faced with countless alternatives regarding which profession to choose, where to live, what college to attend—the list goes on and on. And no doubt the biggest question of all is, Should I plan to get married?

To Marry or Not to Marry?

Based on the number of single people I have spoken

to, I've discovered that the unmarried person's lifestyle is often complicated and frustrating. That was never God's intention.

> But I want you to be free from concern.
> One who is unmarried is concerned about the
> things of the Lord, how he [or she] may please
> the Lord (1 Corinthians 7:32 NASB).

Paul felt strongly that the single life was best. Time, talents and resources can be directed toward the Lord without interference. No outside attachments hinder a life that is free to be directed by the Holy Spirit. Although, like Paul, there are singles who have devoted their lives to Christ with no intention of ever "tying the knot," these individuals are rare and definitely the exception. God has a great and mighty work available for such "specialized" soldiers on the battlefield of life.

But the fact is, a vast majority of single people still desire to be married, and the years leading up to marriage are crucial ones. If your time of preparation for partnership isn't handled properly—spiritually, emotionally, mentally and physically—your eventual marriage can be adversely affected, sometimes with disastrous results.

I have had many single women tell me, "I'm not sure if I can get married because I don't know if I can submit to a husband." Meanwhile, I've yet to hear a single man say, "I'm not sure if I can get married because I don't know if I'll be able to lead my wife and family." Both instances reflect a distorted concept about headship and submission. If, because you're single, you've just skipped to this chapter, it's essential that you go back and read chapters

2 and 3. They will give you a clearer understanding of submission in a broader sense.

Single people are called to submit to God's Word, their pastors, their parents (when they're living at home), their employers and the authorities in the land. The degree to which they are willing to yield in those circumstances will be reflected in their ability to submit to God's plan for marriage. Oddly enough, some people think that once their vows have been said, they'll be able to soar immediately and effortlessly into the responsibilities of headship and submission. No wonder we have so many crashes!

As Oprah Winfrey filled her studio with soon-to-be-wed couples for our appearance on her television show, Frank and I couldn't help but notice that the room contained more than its share of misinformed men and women. If there were a red stamp that said "Divorce Guaranteed," it probably would have been imprinted across a large percentage of the engaged couples in attendance there. A lot of them were clearly "independent thinkers." And most of them were headed for trouble!

Submission is an attitude that extends from single life into married life. It does not begin the day you're married; it begins now. And it plays an integral part in everything you do.

Developing Submission Muscles

Submission, like a muscle, can be strong or weak depending on the amount of exercise it receives. A single person's submissive muscles should be as strong as those of married men and women.

And just how are these submission "muscles" really

developed in singles? Well, for one thing, they *don't* develop when the individual exercises the option of retreating whenever things get too difficult. If a relationship becomes bothersome, singles can always escape for a few days to "cool off." Not so in marriage—neither leadership nor submission is matured by escape!

One of the "muscle-building" suggestions I make to singles is to become accountable to a group of Christians who are walking closely with the Lord. These men and/or women should be studying God's Word, attending a Bible-based church and exemplifying Christ in their lives. By being accountable to others for personal actions and decisions, and by having others accountable to them, unmarried people experience new and invigorating challenges.

For the past 13 years, I have been meeting with a small group of women—single and married—once a week for two hours. Our meeting has no agenda.

It is not a Bible study, although we use our Bibles. It is not a prayer meeting, although we pray. It is a group of women motivated to walk together in committed relationships. We represent several denominations, and our bond is Jesus Christ. We do our best to allow the Holy Spirit to guide our time together, and we share freely and openly from our hearts.

There have been several times when various relationships have become strained, but we're determined to work through problems together, finding suitable solutions. Now and then a visitor attends. We quickly explain our purpose for being together because it can be quite shocking to an outsider when we begin holding each other accountable. But the results speak for themselves: The completion of this book is largely due to the persistent concern of my invaluable friends.

A recent incident exemplifies the pain and blessing of being responsible to others and submitting one to another. Let me tell you about a single woman in our fellowship—we'll call her JoAnn.

A Lesson in Accountability

We were halfway through one of our restaurant meetings when JoAnn hurriedly rounded a corner and headed toward our table. Since we were deep in conversation, we gave her a courteous acknowledgment and returned to our discussion.

Toward the end of the luncheon, JoAnn made what at first appeared to be some casual comments. She said, "You know, sometimes it's difficult just to know where to go and what to do. Recently, I met a man named James at the spa and we got to talking. He's got some problems and I want to help him.

"After we met, I remembered what we talked about here at fellowship a few weeks ago...about getting a brother to counsel a brother. But since I couldn't find anyone, I've been encouraging him in the Word myself. I need your prayers."

One of the women gently asked, "Are you becoming romantically involved?" JoAnn's surprised expression indicated that she wasn't expecting that very strategic question!

She hesitantly replied, "Well, you could say that it's becoming that way." As she began to share more and more about the young man, red flags went up all over the room!

We were all well aware of JoAnn's personal circumstances. Beautiful, witty and energetic for the Lord, she had been waiting for a long time for the man God had for her. Her dream of a big family was being challenged daily, for each birthday brought her closer to 40.

Knowing all this was of deep concern to JoAnn, one by one the women shared their own misgivings about James. JoAnn began to weep. She went on to tell us how her roommate had begun a relationship with a man, and every day when JoAnn came home, he was there. Not only was he there but, as often as not, he and her roommate were locked in a heated embrace. She sobbed, "I want someone to hold me, too! I want someone to listen and care about me. And James, for all his faults, has been filling that void in my life."

So within two weeks (she had missed the previous week's fellowship), in a vulnerable state of mind, JoAnn had met someone and was beginning to "fall in love." We advised her that the friendship certainly didn't appear to be God's best for her. One of the women promised to give James' name to her husband, asking him to assist with the man's spiritual needs. JoAnn agreed, but her eyes revealed that she felt she knew James' needs best.

Would JoAnn find the strength to give him up? She said she would.

That same evening, I saw her at a meeting. As she was going out the door she said over her shoulder, "Pray for James! He's in jail!" I thought to myself, "Boy, it's a good thing that's over."

The next week we were talking on the telephone when JoAnn mentioned that she had visited James in jail. Then she told me that his ex-wife had somehow found her apartment, and had arrived uninvited to tell her everything James had ever done wrong. It was obvious by her tone, that she hadn't believed the ugly report. I could sense that her loyalty to James was deepening.

I was frustrated! I firmly asked her, "JoAnn, what are you doing?"

"What do you mean?"

"All this time," I replied, "you have been waiting for God's best in your life. You've been in prayer, active in God's work, and now all of a sudden you're holding a conversation with me about a man's ex-wife coming to your apartment, and you're visiting your prospective boyfriend in jail! The fellowship admonished you about the dangers of pursuing your association with James, but you keep developing it. I'm confused! JoAnn, I really believe you're being 'set up' by the enemy. You need to end this relationship!"

Irritation sharpened her voice, and we exchanged only a few more words before she hung up the phone. I deeply pondered whether I had said the right things. Then I whispered a prayer to the Lord to hit a straight line with a crooked stick.

Sunday morning, JoAnn wasn't in church. My heart sank to my stomach. That evening when I saw her, she walked up to me and whispered, "I did it."

"Did what?" I was almost afraid to ask!

"I went to the jail today and ended the relationship

with James." As I reached out to embrace her, she whispered, "Please don't. I'll start to cry."

JoAnn had submitted to the guidance of the fellowship. When I asked her several weeks later how she was, she responded, "I've totally surrendered James to the Lord. I hardly ever think about him. When I do, I just begin to pray for him. I'm free!"

Just recently she has met a gentleman for whom I know she's glad she waited. I wonder where JoAnn would be today if she hadn't been accountable to some sisters who love her and want the best for her. She will be able to carry that same accountability over into her marriage. Many of the challenges of submission in marriage will have already been rehearsed within our fellowship!

Submission and the Church

This same sort of growth also occurs within the local church as singles learn to respond positively to the biblical order there. The church is a body of believers who follow the teachings of Jesus Christ. Just as it is natural for avid football, baseball and basketball fans to flock to their favorite games, so believers who love the Lord enjoy coming together at a church gathering. Their desire is to praise and worship the Lord while edifying and encouraging one another.

Before Jesus was crucified and raised from the dead, He prayed a prayer to the Father about His followers:

> I do not ask in behalf of these alone, but
> for those also who believe in Me through their
> word; that they may all be one; even as Thou,

Father, art in Me, and I in Thee, that they also
may be in Us; that the world may believe that
Thou didst send Me (John 17:20,21 NASB).

How is it possible for the church to become one when
it is made up of so many different personalities and opinions? Did Jesus pray in vain? No! He proved to us that
"oneness" could be accomplished through His relationship with the Father. He operated according to God's
established order. And, to this very day, if unity is going
to be accomplished in the church, it will be done through
submission.

The established order for the church is that we first
submit to God and then to the pastor:

Submit yourselves therefore to God (James
4:7).

Obey them that have the rule over you,
and submit yourselves; for they watch for
your souls, as they that must give account,
that they may do it with joy and not with
grief; for that is unprofitable for you (Hebrews
13:17).

According to Scripture, our pastors will one day give an
account to God for what we've all done under their leadership. God encourages us to submit so that the report
may be given in joy and not with grief.

A Serious Choice

Because Satan has deceived Jesus Christ's followers,

many of us do not understand how serious a decision we make when we join a church. It is not unusual for a person to say that he selected his church for one of the following reasons:

1. It is close to home.
2. The service is only an hour long.
3. I like the choir.
4. The church has a strong youth department.
5. My family has gone there for 50 years.

However, when we look at God's established order between pastor and congregation, we realize that a bit more needs to be considered. If we join a particular church, we are called to submit to the pastor's leadership. If we do not agree with the way things are run or the doctrines that are taught, if we begin to murmur and complain or grow rebellious and stubborn, we violate God's commandments. Eventually, we will have to deal with the consequences of that sin.

Can you imagine for a moment the spirit that would exist in a church where all the members are one with the pastor as he diligently seeks God's face? That's not to suggest that the pastor will always make the right decisions. But suppose he has a congregation that never criticizes, and chooses only to pray for him?

When we walk into the church, there is a sweet and warm spirit that permeates the sanctuary. At the end of the service, the only words we hear are those of praise: praise to God, praise of the pastor, praise of the other believers. Sounds like a taste of heaven, doesn't it? But it can happen right here on earth when the principle of submission is in operation.

Submitting to your pastor is the right choice. Single men and women can be used effectively when they have committed their time, talents and resources to the local church under the authority of their pastor. They have the freedom to arrange their schedules to be available for the Lord's work. And, should they eventually desire to get married, they will have vigorously exercised their submission muscles by yielding to the Lord and to the pastor He has placed over His people.

The Barometer

Every area of existence has a positive and negative side, and so it is with the single life. Being single can be deceptive. If a single person gets angry about something, she (or he) can go home, slam the door and scream at the walls for three days straight. After the storm subsides, the individual can pray, "Lord, forgive me. I acted like a child. I am truly sorry I got angry because I know You were offended. Help me to be victorious if that situation arises again."

That's it—end of problem! In movie-making jargon, "That's a wrap!" First John 1:9 says,

> If we confess our sins, he is faithful and
> just to forgive us our sins, and to cleanse us
> from all unrighteousness.

It's easy for single persons who have surrendered their lives to God to feel they have everything well in hand when they get married. They've been practicing submission with the Lord.

There's only one problem: Your mate won't be perfect! Even if he loves the Lord, I doubt if he'll be willing to tolerate your running upstairs, slamming doors and screaming. When you finally apologize, instead of receiving forgiveness, you may end up with the cold shoulder. Being married puts a mirror in front of you daily and gives you little time to adjust. This can be to your advantage.

One of the reasons I enjoy being married is that my home life is a constant barometer that tells me where I am in the Lord. I can't have stormy weather with Frank and sunshine with God. Peace in my relationship with God is dependent on maintaining a submissive spirit with my husband. So I'm learning to make my adjustments quickly—a skill it took me eight years of marriage to develop.

Until married persons accept having that barometer around all the time, they struggle to maintain their equilibrium. Like one woman said about her new Christian husband, "I just didn't expect him to be so carnal"—in other words: human!

Choosing Friends Carefully

Marriage may or may not be in God's plans for you. However, He would have you submit to His Word as you develop relationships, especially those involving the opposite sex. Many acquaintances will cross your path, but only a few will develop into relationships. Webster's

Dictionary defines "relationship" as "the state of being related or interrelated." That sort of bond is not casual.

Whether the person you meet is male or female, you should study each person carefully: 1. Is he (or she) walking in the light? 2. How does she (or he) make decisions?

> But you are a chosen race, a royal priesthood, a holy nation, a people for God's own possession, that you may proclaim the excellencies of Him who has called you out of darkness into His marvelous light (1 Peter 2:9 NASB).

Every now and then you will probably be drawn to certain individuals and will want to know them better. Something about them is special. You feel they can add another dimension to your life. And maybe they can—if, that is, they can pass the "Light" test!

> God is light and in Him is no darkness at all. If we say that we have fellowship with Him and walk in darkness, we lie and do not practice the truth; but if we walk in the light as He Himself is in the light, we have fellowship with one another (1 John 1:5-7 NASB).

In new relationships, one thing most of us fail to do is listen. We become so busy sharing whatever is on our own minds that we forget to concentrate on the response. I once heard someone say, "If you let a person talk for 15 minutes without interruption, he'll tell you what is most important in his life."

It's always amazing to me when I ask a single woman who has been dating a man for weeks, "Does he know the Lord?" most of the time the response is either, "We haven't gotten around to talking about that," or "Well, he believes in God but I'm not sure where he stands with Jesus."

A person who walks "in the Light" speaks of "the Light." Some people might suggest, "Bunny, there's more to talk about in life than Jesus," and I totally agree. I'm simply talking about priorities. "What is your relationship with Jesus Christ?" should top our list of "getting-to-know-you" questions. If Jesus is the first consideration in our lives, then He will also be the first thing we want to talk about.

If you love the Lord, His light will shine through you and others will either be drawn to you or driven away. Darkness hates the light. If your new friends belong to the darkness, the only way you can proceed with the relationship is to turn down or switch off your light, and that can never be a wise move.

I believe 2 Corinthians 6:14 says it best:

> Be ye not unequally yoked together with unbelievers; for what fellowship hath righteousness with unrighteousness? and what communion hath light with darkness?

Don't be deceived! Unbelievers may be articulate in thought and speech, but their opinions emanate out of darkness. The more close, personal time you spend with them, the more shadows they will cast across your life.

Dating God's Way

And while we're on the subject of trying to mix darkness and light, let's consider one of the most difficult instructions God has given to single men and women:

> For this is the will of God, even your sanctification, that ye should abstain from fornication (1 Thessalonians 4:3).

Single women have told me countless stories about dating Christian men who refuse to submit to God's Word in this sensitive area.

Their rebuttal to the Scripture is, "C'mon. God knows we're only human. He'll understand because He's the one who gave us these desires." Of course, in some instances it's the woman, not the man, who makes this kind of statement. In either case, failure to submit to God in sexuality can cause serious consequences in marriage.

What is actually being cultivated is a spirit of rebellion. And, once they're on the other side of the altar, it will come back to haunt the rebels. No sooner do we say, "I do," than we are faced with another Scripture to which God also expects us to submit:

> The wife hath not power of her own body, but the husband; and likewise also the husband hath not power of his own body, but the wife. Defraud ye not one the other, except it be with consent for a time, that ye may give yourselves to fasting and prayer; and come together again, that Satan tempt you not for your incontinency (1 Corinthians 7:4,5).

The same spirit of rebellion that demands sex before marriage will refuse sex after marriage! Sexually active unmarried couples are unknowingly generating and cultivating a defiance against God. That willfulness will have far-reaching effects in the years to come.

That brings up an intriguing puzzle. Which is most difficult: being single and having to abstain from sex or being married and having to submit your body when you don't feel like it? (One single woman naively asked me, "Who wouldn't want to?") I'm sure if you give this serious consideration, you will say that the latter is actually more difficult. And so it is that God's first commandment appears to be preparing us to obey the second!

But perhaps the most disturbing aspect of this entire debate is this: If a man wants to break God's laws before you are married, how on earth can you trust him to take over the leadership of your life afterward? If a woman refuses to submit to God's ordinances before she's married, how can you expect her to yield to your leadership decisions once you're married?

When It Comes to Decisions…

That brings us to another important point. How does your new friend presently make personal decisions: by seeking the mind of God or by depending on cleverness and self-reliance?

You'll often meet people who seem to have all the answers. If they happen to be successful, you may genuinely admire them and crave their company. After all, "winners" seem to have so much to offer. But are they spiritually victorious? That's an altogether different matter. God's Word challenges us to:

> Trust in the Lord with all your heart, and do not lean on your own understanding. In all your ways acknowledge Him, and He will make your paths straight (Proverbs 3:5,6 NASB).

A person who walks in the light knows that he is finite and that he is dealing with an infinite God.

> For my thoughts are not your thoughts, neither are your ways my ways, saith the Lord (Isaiah 55:8).

Whenever we become interrelated with other people, we are affected by the way they think, rationalize and make choices. Our spiritual health depends on our communion with people of like mind who love the Lord and desire to do His will.

Sometimes I wish I could put up a roadblock, guarded with heavily armed personnel, that every unmarried woman who's husband-hunting would have to pass through. As she pulled to a stop, her relationships with the opposite sex would be inspected, and a bright light would be shined into her eyes.

The interrogator would ask, "Have you considered the fact that once you marry this man you're going to have to submit to his judgment for the rest of your life? Do you understand that 'till death do you part' you're going to have to follow his leadership?"

Most women do not realize the seriousness of their

decision to marry. Caught up in the romance and thrill of it all, they often neglect to notice that they are willingly and permanently turning over the reins of their lives. Unless a husband is asking a wife to do something immoral, she is required by God's Word to follow his leadership. And if the man is not getting his direction from the Lord, the wife will spend the rest of her life going in whatever direction his earthly, unspiritual mind dictates.

Here's a tip: A person who is following God's leading will share his thoughts and will let you know he is praying over his choices. Rejoice if he asks you to join him in prayer! If he does, you'll know you have a good, godly relationship developing.

Taking Wise Precautions

After approaching budding relationships carefully and prayerfully, I encourage all single people to take a marriage enrichment class *before* they get married. Since the husband is the head of the wife, if he decides they don't need counseling once they're married, they won't be able to go. By then, they find themselves struggling all alone with many challenges that could have been handled before they ever said their vows.

Four "war zones" that most frequently create battles in marriage are sex, communication, finances and in-laws. Every one of these concerns should be thoroughly discussed and intelligently addressed before anyone walks down an aisle. The only obstacle to that kind of preparation is that "young lovers" are often blinded by emotion. "Love conquers all," they tell themselves. Often as not, they don't realistically address the very issues that can ultimately do untold damage to that precious love.

Remember the age-old proverb: "An ounce of prevention is worth a pound of cure." Take a realistic look at married life—*now!*

The Single Parent

While researching submission and the single person, I talked to dozens of unmarried friends and counselees. I also made a point of calling some friends of mine who are single parents. I asked about their joys and frustrations.

It wasn't long before I realized that being a "single" and being a single parent are two very different matters. We have a tendency to put all singles into one box. The lid won't shut, but we sit on the box and try to force a perfect fit anyway. Not one of the burdens my single-parent friends discussed with me paralleled those of unmarried women and men.

Single parents don't have the support of the complete family unit, nor do they have the freedom of a single person. To quote one woman, "I feel displaced. I'm not included with married couples because I don't have a husband, and it's difficult to relate to single people because our focus is different. Every decision I make starts and ends with the children. There is subtle pressure placed on you to remarry, and everything you do is viewed by others with that in mind. It really impedes my effectiveness in ministering to others."

How does a single parent apply submission to his or her life? The same way a single person does, but with one significant difference: The children must be taught by leadership and by example. In order to prepare children to submit to authority, single parents must not only enforce submission in the home (not always easy when only one parent is present), but also practice it in their own lives. They should teach their children what they're doing and why they're doing it. Gary Richmond's excellent book *Successful Single Parenting* (Harvest House), deals with many of these issues in clear and concise detail.

As we've said before, submission is a principle that affects every aspect of our lives. When a decision is made that goes against your will but demonstrates your submission to God's Word, if it's appropriate, let your children know. Be honest and forthright with them, allowing them to understand how difficult compliance can be for you. By observation they will learn and will be able to transfer a yielded attitude into their own lives.

Ye Are the Salt

Submission is essential to a single person. It's the hub that turns the wheel in all of our relationships. It's as invigorating as an aerobics class and as stimulating as the shower that follows. But more than that, submission in your life sets a precedent for all who know you, who recognize your faith in the Lord Jesus and who observe your conduct.

> Ye are the salt of the earth; but if the salt have lost his savour, wherewith shall it be salted? It is thenceforth good for nothing, but to be cast out, and to be trodden under foot of

men. Ye are the light of the world. A city that is set on an hill cannot be hid....Let your light so shine before men, that they may see your good works and glorify your Father which is in heaven (Matthew 5:13-16).

This world needs more single people who are submissive—and have the faith to prove it!

Chapter 9

Some Single-Minded
Questions

⌐

Q.

I am dating someone about whom I have deep
feelings. He says that since we're getting married
someday, that God will forgive us if we have sexual
intercourse. How can I submit to God's teaching
when I don't want to resist him?

A.

Ask yourself the question, "Do I want God's
grace for me or God's best for me?" Your fiancé is

correct—God will forgive you. However, you will reap the harvest of your disobedience.

If he continues to pressure you, you may need to take a closer look at this individual you intend to marry. If you're both Christians, he should be more sensitive to God's commandments and His leading. Although you have deep feelings, he may not be someone to whom you should entrust the leadership of your home.

Q.

Before I became a Christian, if someone asked me to go out and I didn't want to be bothered, I just said "No!" Now I feel so guilty. I'm aware that the person God has for me may not seem like "my type," at least not at first. However, I just can't date everyone who asks. What do I do or say? Help!

A.

A man once told me, "I'm afraid to let God pick out my mate because I probably won't agree with His taste." Let's begin by asking some relevant questions.

First of all, why do you date? Some singles are earnestly looking for a mate. Others simply want to have fellowship with the opposite sex. If marriage is all you're really interested in, then your standards will be very specific.

You'll want to find out what you can about your prospective mate before you spend a great deal of time with him. Certainly godliness and Christian commitment will top your list of "must-haves." Beyond that, is he a) sincere, b) moral, c) trustworthy, and d) suitable? If you are really serious about no casual dates, you may even want to explain that you're long past being interested in casual relationships.

One way of keeping this perspective is by going out in a group so that you can observe people without being pressured. Group fellowship is the safest environment for easing into meaningful relationships. Without stress or strain, you can decide if one person or another deserves your serious consideration.

If you're only looking for casual fellowship with the opposite sex, you may want to consider your motives. Many single Christians date the opposite sex because they are insecure, lonely and need attention and kind words from others who consider them attractive and interesting. Emotional neediness is a vulnerable position from which to operate. Getting attention and "strokes" can be fun, yes. But bear in mind that personal fulfillment should first come from a satisfying relationship with the Lord. Any other validation is man's opinion, which could possibly be tainted by ulterior motives.

I personally suggest if couples are going out casually that each person pays his own way. This keeps obligation out of the picture, and no one expects anything "in return" for a good dinner, a concert seat or a theater ticket.

Q.

My parents want to control my life. I think that if I were married it would be easier for me to assert my right to make my own decisions. I know that we're called to love and honor our parents, but I don't know where to draw the line.

A.

You can help draw the line by first determining where you're going with your life. What are your goals? What are your plans? After you have thought through these questions, write down your answers and hold a family meeting. Let your parents know how much you love them. Explain that you want them to know about the decisions you've made for your life.

Give your mother and father an opportunity to express themselves regarding your direction. Listen to them with careful consideration. Let them know you will pray about all they say, and once you're sure of your course, give them your decision. Stand firm and be willing to accept the credit or blame for whatever you've decided.

Giving parents a solid plan for the future helps them understand that their baby has grown up.

Q.

At my church, singles are treated like second-class citizens. I love my pastor and I'm committed to my church, but I don't know how to get our leaders to realize that we need special programs too. What approach should I take?

A.

The first approach to anything should be prayer and a consecrated heart and mind. Unfortunately, humans are creatures of habit. We usually stick to tradition and are most comfortable when things are status quo. Perhaps your pastor has never been a part of a singles ministry and doesn't quite know how to develop it.

When I need Frank's help on a plan that I have, once I've prayed it through, I put my thoughts on paper and have him review it. Then he simply has to make adjustments rather than to initiate a new program.

After you have prayed, present your pastor with a workable and viable plan for the singles in your church. Even if he reconstructs the format, you have at least begun moving in the right direction. If your pastor is anything like mine, it may take some time before he makes a decision. Still, you can be comforted in knowing that it's on his mind.

Q.

My girlfriend doesn't know the Lord; however, I'm believing that God is going to save her. Some of my Christian friends say that I am playing with fire, but I just can't see it. What do you advise?

A.

If you had said that she was a casual acquaintance, I might have agreed with you. But the mere fact that you use the term "girlfriend" means that you are already emotionally involved with her. One of the greatest tools that Satan uses in our lives is emotions. Many Christians base their lives on how they feel rather than on what God's Word says.

So I have a question for you. What does God's Word say about the relationship you're in? The first Scripture that comes to mind is Amos 3:3: "Can two walk together, except they be agreed?"

If we are believers in Jesus Christ, our number-one aim in life should be to "love the Lord thy God with all thy heart, and with all thy soul, and with all thy strength" (Mark 12:30).

That should place Him first in all thoughts and conversations *and* relationships!

Recently, a friend of mine impulsively married an unsaved man. Her statement to me was, "I know that God will save him." That may be so, but one big question is, When? Not only that, after he becomes saved she will have to deal with a baby Christian—a man who will just be beginning to understand what Christ expects of his life.

When she asked me if I thought she had made a mistake, I answered, "Yes." I went on to explain that he could well have been the man for her. The mistake may not be that he was the wrong man. It may just have been the wrong time.

Somehow, we seem to think that if we can keep the loved one close to us, he (or she) will be influenced to make a decision. That's manipulation. Once we're married, God gives instructions about how to bear witness for Him with an unsaved mate. But when we defy the Scriptures in order to suit our willful needs and desires, then we'd better be ready to pay the consequences, which can be very painful indeed.

Second Corinthians 6:14 says, "Be ye not unequally yoked." God would have to go against His own Word to bless the marriage of an unsaved person to one of His children. When your friends said you were playing with fire, they were absolutely correct.

Jesus once said that before we're born again, "Ye are of your father the devil." If you decide to marry this girl, don't be surprised if you meet up with your father-in-law!

Q.

I hate my job. My boss has a weak character. He continually asks me to do things that I don't feel God would be pleased with. Do I have to submit when I'm asked to do something I believe to be wrong?

A.

The answer to that is a resounding "No!" A woman once shared a testimony with me regarding a similar situation.

Susan went to work as a receptionist/secretary for a land development company. Her boss was obnoxious. When people called, he would yell at her from his office, "Tell them I'm not in!" She did that a few times, then kindly told him that lying about his whereabouts compromised her beliefs and that she could no longer do it.

He became irate. Just then the phone rang. When she told him who was calling, he shouted, "Tell them I'm not in!" She picked up the phone and said, "One moment please, he's right here."

As soon as he had slammed down the telephone, he came storming out to her desk. No sooner had he arrived, the telephone rang again. When she informed him about the caller, he spoke through clenched teeth and hissed, "Tell her I'm not in."

She looked him squarely in the eyes and said, "If you want me to tell her you're not in, then you're going to have to leave!"

He glared at her for a moment. When he realized that she was serious, he stomped out of the office and stood outside, in front of the swinging glass doors.

She got up from behind her desk, opened the door slightly and announced, "No! If you want me to tell them you're not here, then you'll have to get in your car and drive away."

Guess what he did? He got in his car and drove away.

Once he returned, he did two things: First, he got mad. Then, not long thereafter, he got saved!

When we ask God for a job, it's not unusual for Him to select a place for us where a Christian warrior's presence is required. We have a tendency to think that God would never put us in a uncomfortable position. But that's not the issue. God doesn't need to give us a job to provide for us—He's able to rain manna from the sky. The Lord wants us to "occupy until He comes," to stand against the gates of hell and to continue to pull down strongholds.

Q.

My boss is a pain! Our personalities are incompatible. I don't like submitting to her, and yet I need my job too much to quit. What should I do?

A.

I know very well that bosses can be difficult. But God didn't place you where you are so you could have a great time every day. You, in essence, are a missionary at your job. That means you're working with heathens whom Christ loves, setting a godly example for them.

Here's a portion of a letter I received from a woman who had to repent from being unsubmissive to her boss. Notice what God did to take care of His child.

> On Monday I saw my boss. She told me she was going to the field and she'd see me tomorrow. I said, "Ilene,

before you go, I have to apologize to you. I have not been submissive to you. I'm really sorry."

She looked puzzled because we'd had so many problems. Mrs. Wilson, you pointed out that the boss may be right or wrong but we are to be submissive anyway. So I apologized.

The following Monday morning, just a week later, Ilene gave me a promotion. She gave me a higher position paying $13,000 more a year than I was making! Praise God. Soon thereafter God opened doors for us to buy a new home, including the funds. I give all the praise to the Lord.

Do you see what God can do? While you're asking Him to give you the grace to submit, ask Him to give you wisdom as to how He can use you to turn your entire office around. All He needs is someone who is willing. He'll take care of the rest.

Q.

I'll be the first to admit that I'm not a beautiful woman. To top it all off, I'm shy. I would love to get married and raise a family, but the possibility of someone asking me out is slim to none. Can you help me?

A.

I'm sure you have heard all the clichés such as "Beauty is in the eyes of the beholder" and "Beauty is only skin deep." We live in a world surrounded by "beautiful people." There is a woman who has had a profound impact on my life. She attends my church and is the mother of five children.

Soft-spoken and gentle in demeanor, Gwen was burned badly as a little child. Her face was damaged beyond repair, and yet she is one of the most enjoyable people I have ever met. One day I had the opportunity to work with her in our church nursery. I was compelled to ask her how she was burned. After telling me the story, I wanted to know how it had affected her life.

She said that her life was better for it. She had an opportunity to see the world as it really is. It amazes her that people see only outer beauty. She said, "I have heard beautiful people speak and, although everyone listened intently, they really didn't say anything! It takes twice as long for people to hear what I have to say, but when I'm done they know they've really heard something."

A few years ago, she had the opportunity to get her face repaired through modern medicine. Just before her surgery, she asked the Lord what He thought. He told her He loved her and wanted to use her just the way she was. She canceled the surgery. Now Gwen wants to teach other people what God's taught her about having a healthy self-image.

It's been said that self-image is not how other people see you, but how you *think* they see you. In the Song of Solomon, the Shulamite woman felt that she was unattractive because that was what she'd always heard from her brothers. It took the king to convince her that through his eyes she was the fairest in the land. Of course, he had to tell her over and over again. Once she finally accepted it, her countenance was transformed in such a way that even her brothers didn't recognize her.

I suggest you involve yourself in areas where you come into direct and constant contact with people. The special qualities God has given you will shine through, and the mate God has prepared for you will love you just the way you are. And perhaps most important of all, ask God to give you the desires of your heart. He has promised to place His desire within you (Psalm 37), and He has committed Himself to provide for your every need. I personally believe that includes emotional needs, too.

I'm a Christian single and very active in my church. Because I'm not married and accountable to a mate, I find myself overextended in many areas. To tell you the truth, I have difficulty determining which responsibilities and activities are the ones God wants me to be doing. How can I tell?

A.

That is a very real challenge in the life of a single person; in fact, it is a consideration for all Christians.

One day I made plans to conduct an important evening meeting about an hour away from home. I called several people and asked them to meet me there. When everything was arranged, I realized that I had not told Frank my plans. When I called him at his office, he quickly informed me that he felt the decision was unwise and that he wanted me to find someone to go in my place.

I immediately rebelled! I tried to convince him that it was imperative for me to go. He stood his ground and I submitted. As I began making calls, a couple came to mind that would be perfect for making the presentation. When I contacted them, it just happened that they were going to be in that particular city that evening. They made the presentation and were much more effective than I would have been.

The situation was excruciatingly painful. I had to swallow my pride in order to give in to Frank's decision. But he was right. The whole thing was really too much for me. And had I been single, I would have overextended myself, even though I would have been doing the "right thing."

As we discussed before, a single person needs

to be accountable to some Christian brothers and/or sisters. It's important that these friends are people who don't always agree with you, who will challenge your decisions when you appear to be going off course. Even if they are not always right, the relationships will cause you to pause and contemplate concerns you may not have considered.

Being accountable to others will also help prolong your response time when you're asked to do something. When you say, "I'll pray and get back to you," it gives you the space to call your friends and get their advice, even in matters that seem small. If they are not in agreement, pray a little longer and make sure you have God's approval.

Chapter 10

A Will in the Middle of a Will

By now I hope we all better understand the principle of submission. And I hope you've accepted God's call to submit. Now let me explain to you how you can get started. Are you ready?

In two words: *You can't!*

The Tug-of-War

Our human will is repelled by the thought of not being

in control. It wars against God's will for our lives. The
flesh is constantly looking for a hiding place from the
bright glare of submission. The war between our flesh
and the Spirit will be continuous.

> For the flesh lusteth against the Spirit,
> and the Spirit against the flesh; and these
> are contrary the one to the other; so that ye
> cannot do the things that ye would (Galatians
> 5:17).

So there we have it—all-out anarchy. My pastor says
that the Spirit and the flesh are like two dogs fighting.
Whichever one you want to win, that's the one you feed.
We must feed the inner man to withstand the strategies
of the enemy. Ephesians 3:16-19 says:

> That he would grant you, according to the
> riches of his glory, to be strengthened with
> might by his Spirit in the inner man; that
> Christ may dwell in your hearts by faith; that
> ye, being rooted and grounded in love, may
> be able to comprehend with all the saints
> what is the breadth, and length, and depth,
> and height; and to know the love of Christ,
> which passeth knowledge, that ye might be
> filled with all the fulness of God.

Being submissive cannot be accomplished apart from
walking in the Spirit.

> This I say then, walk in the Spirit, and ye

shall not fulfil the lust of the flesh (Galatians
5:16).

Safe in Him

Walking in the Spirit is putting your total faith in
Jesus Christ, confessing your sins as they appear, and
moving forward with faith that they have been forgiven.
It's like being in a bubble that has been inflated with
love, joy, peace, longsuffering, gentleness, goodness, faith,
meekness and self-control. Attached to the bubble is a
cord that is connected to the Lord. As He communicates
with us, He sends forth His wisdom, knowledge and
understanding.

This bubble allows us to bounce back and forth between
life's challenges and difficulties. It doesn't eliminate them,
it just insulates us from experiencing the same impact
that is felt by those who are attempting to handle them
on their own.

When we do things independently of God, the bubble
breaks and our fellowship (not our relationship) with God
is broken. We are now walking in the flesh. It's during
this time that we are the most vulnerable to making rash
decisions and bad judgments. We respond out of frustration, not love. How do we get back in the bubble once it's
been broken? First John 1:9 says:

If we confess our sins, he is faithful and
just to forgive us our sins, and to cleanse us
from all unrighteousness.

When we sincerely repent of our sins, the Lord forgives

us and fellowship is restored. That's why praying for forgiveness can't wait until we go to bed at night. It has to be continuous throughout the day so that we can stay in constant fellowship with the Father.

The Holy Spirit is one with the Father and always seeks to do His will. Jesus participates in that oneness also: "I do always those things that please him [the Father]" (John 8:29).

Jesus was totally submitted to the Father, no matter what God asked Him to do. In the Garden of Gethsemane, we remember Jesus saying,

> O my Father, if it be possible, let this cup pass from me; nevertheless, not as I will, but as thou wilt (Matthew 26:39).

Our submission to God and our fellowman will never require Christ's degree of agony and brokenness—certainly not to the actual "sweating of blood." However, we surely face our own miniature Gardens of Gethsemane every day of our lives—places where our wills cross God's will.

I believe the greatest war stories are not found in history books but in the lives of Christians struggling to be obedient to God's will. To outsiders, the challenges we face may seem minuscule. To us, they are often larger than life.

Some may laugh at my "tea story," but on the day it took place, my agonizing would have toppled the Richter scale.

The Tempest and the Teacup

As Frank and I came to the end of our day and were in the bedroom, from his reclining position on the bed he said, "Honey, would you get me a cup of hot tea?"

I replied, "Sure."

After I had closed the door softly and headed down the stairs, my anger began to surge and swell. I thought to myself, "Why do I have to get the tea? Why can't he make me a cup of tea? After all, I've been just as busy as he has. I've been out running errands, taking care of children, cleaning the house and so many other things I can't even count them all!" The more I thought about it, the more livid I became.

I leaned against the stove waiting for the water to boil and whispered a silent prayer: "Lord, I know that the Bible says that against You and You alone have I sinned. I also know that when I sin it causes the Holy Spirit to grieve and the Holy Spirit is You. Please God, I don't want to grieve You, but I am so angry that unless You show me how to get out of this, I don't know what I'll say or do when I get upstairs. I'm disgusted!"

As I uttered the prayer, the Holy Spirit replied. He began with asking the question, "Do you remember the Scripture: 'Consider others better than yourselves' (Philippians 2:3 NIV)?"

I mentally nodded my head and He continued, "What about God's desire when He said:

> Ye have heard that it hath been said,
> Thou shalt love thy neighbour, and hate
> thine enemy; but I say unto you, Love your

enemies, bless them that curse you, do good to them that hate you, and pray for them which despitefully use you, and persecute you (Matthew 5:43,44)."

My silent reply was, "But I don't hate Frank. I love him!"

The Holy Spirit responded, "Of course you do. And if you can't pull this Scripture off with someone you love, do you think you could ever do it with someone who hates you?"

Softly I responded, "No."

But the Holy Spirit had one more comment that caused my defiance to melt. He whispered, "What about the Scripture you memorized last week?"

Whoever wants to become great among you must be your servant, and whoever wants to be first must be your slave (Matthew 20:26 NIV).

It was that Scripture that caused me to weep over the boiling water. My will had crossed God's will in His desire for a healthy marriage. Once again, I had been swept up by the peripheral and ignored God's ultimate goal for our lives—that Frank and I should become one in Him.

When I set the hot tea on the bed stand, Frank said, "Thank you." My answer was simply, "You're welcome, honey." Unbeknown to him, World War III had just taken place in our kitchen! However, the smile on my face came from the fact that even though many people in the world might have considered it a defeat, I knew that I had won.

I was no longer bound by anger and rebellion, but free to love and give.

One reason submission is such a big obstacle is because very few people have—or want to have—a servant's heart. We explain our disservice to one another in the name of equal rights. But when the Holy Spirit blows away that smoke screen, all that remains standing are four proud pillars: arrogance, defiance, disobedience and rebellion.

God is searching for some of His children to volunteer for full-time service—children who are willing to walk in the Spirit, children who desire to love Him with heart, mind, and soul. Second Chronicles 16:9 tells us:

> The eyes of the Lord run to and fro throughout the whole earth, to shew himself strong in the behalf of them whose heart is perfect toward him.

God is looking for children who possess a certain spirit.

> To this man [or woman] will I look, even to him that is poor and of a contrite spirit, and trembleth at my word (Isaiah 66:2).

Poor and Helpless

The word "poor" in Isaiah 66:2 means poor and help-less. Suppose we were to take a seven-year-old boy whose parents had abandoned him, drop him off in the middle of skid row and drive away. The boy is poor but not helpless. He can knock on doors and ask for help, go to a fast-food restaurant and eat off people's plates after they have left or even stand on a corner with a tin cup in his hand.

But if we take a two-year-old boy and leave him in the same place, he is truly poor and helpless. Unless someone comes along and assists him, he will eventually die.

God wants children who *know* they are helpless. Jesus says, "I am the vine and you are the branches. Apart from Me you can do nothing."

When we consider our accomplishments in life, it's hard to swallow the fact that apart from Jesus we are helpless. However, we must consider from what point of view Jesus was speaking. He was fully aware that there are people on earth who do not believe in Him and yet have great earthly success. Jesus was referring to the kingdom in which He operates: the spiritual realm.

When Jesus said that apart from Him we can do nothing, He was referring to the spiritual realm that controls everything around us. We can physically put together a prosperous venture, build a dynamic organization or coordinate a successful event. But only Jesus, through His precious Holy Spirit, can change a person's heart and lead him in another direction.

A husband can submit to God and lead his family in what he feels is the right direction, but only God can penetrate his wife's heart so that she will submit to his leadership. A wife can submit to a man's headship, but only God can motivate and enable her husband to love her as Christ loves the church. As God's children we must realize that we are poor and helpless. We sing a song in church that says, "Father, I stretch my hands to thee, no other help I know, If thou remove thy strength from me [withdraw thyself], whither will I go?"

One morning at a print shop I was waiting my turn to get copies made. An elderly gentleman in front of me was mumbling to himself. I took a seat and noticed a puppy in a dog cage seated next to the chair. Within a few seconds, the old man was telling me a story.

"My son is a doctor," he said. "He used to live in a Communist-held country. Children born out of wedlock were considered a disgrace there, and were treated very cruelly. They were left outdoors and ate from scraps found on the ground. Not to have a father was the worst possible disgrace.

"One day my son noticed a tiny orphaned boy covered with mud and sitting in the street. His heart went out to the child. He took him home, cleaned him up and began raising him as a son.

"Seven years later a coup broke out in the country and my son was asked to leave the country or risk losing his life. He went to get the passports in order and was told that he could not take the adopted boy with him. He tried to convince the authorities, but they refused to provide travel documents.

"My son went home and gave the boy a very strong sedative, put him in a dog cage and went to the airport. There was so much confusion that the ticket agent didn't check the dog cage. Had my son's deception been discovered, they would have killed him. But the boy is now 18 years old and attending a university near here."

That story deeply touched me. I couldn't help but think that Jesus did that very thing for us. He chose us—we did not choose Him. We were covered with sin, but He loved us anyway. He cleaned us up, adopted us, and provided salvation when we were poor and helpless. Unless we're operating in God's Spirit, we continue to be poor and helpless. But with His help "[we] can do all things through Christ which strengtheneth [us]."

A Broken Spirit

God is also looking for children with a broken spirit, those who mourn over their own sins and the sins of others.

Once I asked God to show me an example of a broken spirit. A few days later my daughter, Christy, who was six years old at the time, walked into the breakfast room. I was preparing a large dinner and was seated at the table picking green beans. She did something that displeased me and I responded by saying, "Christy, I have told you before never to do that. I am very disappointed in you! Please don't do it again."

As I mentioned before, I have become accustomed to hearing my children make excuses for their behavior instead of apologizing. But this time it was different.

Christy stood still for a few moments and then disappeared. When she returned, she handed me a torn yellow sheet of paper. On the paper was written, "Der Momy, I dont deserv diner tonit. I am sory. Ples forgiv me. Lov, Christy."

When I looked up and extended my hand to her, she fell into my arms with the most heartrending cry I'd ever heard. She was crying because she had disappointed me.

God spoke to me and said, "That is a broken spirit."

I began thinking of things I'd done that had disappointed God. Sure, I'd always said "I'm sorry." But I'd apologized in a flippant way, as if to say, "You have to forgive me because You said You would in Your Word." Right then and there, I understood the haughtiness of my attitude. And as my little girl wept in my arms, I cried unto the Lord for forgiveness myself.

We can usually come up with a list of excuses for our sins:

- God knows I'm only human.
- I had an unhappy childhood.
- I'm too old to change.
- Nobody's perfect.
- The devil made me do it.

But how many of God's children fall into His arms and weep from their hearts at their sins? God is looking for children with a broken spirit.

Trembles at My Word

When God says He is looking for someone who trembles at His Word, the Scripture literally means a "physical shaking." The trembling comes as a result of our meekness.

Meekness means restrained power. Sure, we can take matters into our own hands and try to fix relationships, circumstances and situations. Yet many times the way we would fix things would not please God, and as we've already discovered, "His ways are not our ways." If we're meek, we choose to restrain our power in order to activate His.

Someone may have done something unkind to you. You would be well within your rights to take revenge in response to their acts. Everything in your flesh says, "Do it! They deserve it!" But the trembling begins as you consider,

> "Avenge not yourselves, but rather give place unto wrath: for it is written, Vengeance is mine; I will repay," saith the Lord (Romans 12:19).

Every time we choose to do things God's way, we have to struggle against our intellect and emotions. But it's worth it because we know we're acting like the kind of children God is pleased with.

Do you believe that there is a God who will one day judge your deeds? Just imagine this: You've been invited to your local movie theater and told that everything you had ever done, thought and said would be shown that day—in wide-screen Technicolor! Admission is free. Even your enemies are invited! How differently would we speak, act or think if we thought we'd be exposed? If the idea of the movie theater makes us squeamish, it's because we are motivated by a deep fear of man.

I think we fear man far more than God. Either that, or we simply don't believe that He really is all-knowing, all-powerful and always with us.

But God's Word says He wants children who are meek, who tremble at His Word. "Look," you might say, "that

was the Old Testament." You're right. What does Jesus
think about that? In Matthew 5:3-5 we find one of Jesus'
first recorded sermons. The first three statements made
were:

> Blessed are the poor in spirit: for theirs
> is the kingdom of heaven. Blessed are they
> that mourn: for they shall be comforted.
> Blessed are the meek: for they shall inherit
> the earth.

Submission is faith that operates in a spirit that is
poor, broken and meek. Jesus had that spirit. So must
we.

A Lesson in Submission

During a recent youth conference, I was painfully
reminded of these very principles. "Breakaway" is the
name of a youth gathering I founded several years ago
for California teenagers. Although the conference is really
one of the loves of my life, after directing it for three years
I stepped down. It now is in the hands of a capable and
competent leader named Don.

Although I'm no longer in leadership, I continue to
attend Breakaway, helping out wherever I can. While
sitting in the opening assembly during our latest conference, I noticed that the praise team wasn't especially
effective. The young men and women shifted around
restlessly as they were led in one unfamiliar song after
another.

How frustrated I felt! The minute the room emptied,

I quickly asked why the music was not coming up to its usual superb standard. I learned that the scheduled praise team had canceled just two days before, and had been hurriedly replaced.

I quickly located the two praise leaders, women who happened to be friends of mine. I told them what I thought they should do. They were very cordial and implemented my suggestions willingly. That night they were a smash! The kids didn't want to stop singing, and I couldn't have been more delighted.

But the next day my joy was turned to sadness. I learned that Don, the director of the conference, hadn't been at all pleased with my behavior. When I talked to him, he kindly explained that some of the conference's leadership had been disturbed by the fact that I'd taken it upon myself to solve the praise music problem without consulting them first.

I was livid! Tears streamed from my eyes as I stormed away.

Minutes later, I found myself sitting on a rock overlooking a bubbling stream, crying out, "Lord, You know I never wanted to give this conference up! I love it! I don't get to participate in it much at all anymore, and then when I do one thing it's the *wrong* thing. It's all so ridiculous! Don never once mentioned how wonderful the praise service was. He never thanked me for solving the problem. All he could think about was the other leaders and how they felt!"

As I continued to cry, the Holy Spirit gently spoke. "Yes, you're right. It was a wonderful praise service. But you were wrong in not checking with those in authority over the conference before you meddled. You violated your own teaching—teaching you know you've received from God's Word. Go quickly and apologize, and go *now*."

I jumped to my feet and ran up the hill. When I found Don, I told him I was sorry. I admitted he was right, and that I should have checked with him before making my own changes. He put his arms around my shoulders as I wept. I knew God was pleased and was ministering to both of us.

Walking on Water

I've had to learn that I cannot submit without totally depending on Christ. But once I've done so, I am free to let His Holy Spirit move through me. John 15:4,5,7 says:

> Abide in me, and I in you. As the branch cannot bear fruit of itself, except it abide in the vine, no more can ye, except ye abide in me. I am the vine, ye are the branches; he that abideth in me, and I in him, the same bringeth forth much fruit; for without me ye can do nothing. If ye abide in me, and my words abide in you, ye shall ask what ye will, and it shall be done unto you.

I once heard this saying: "Fear knocked at the door. Faith answered. No one was there." As you close the back cover of this book, the thought of surrendering and submitting your will to God and those in authority may be overwhelming and even frightening.

If the apostle Peter were sitting next to you, he would

be nodding his head in agreement. How he struggled to submit his strong, capable personality to Jesus. Yet Peter walked on water! And through that experience he quickly learned that because Jesus was with him, he was perfectly safe.

You and I have to cross deep waters of uncertainty. What will happen if we step out of our own will and venture out in faith, submitting and trusting? Will we sink? No, my friend. Once we're willing to leave the boat and fix our eyes on Him, Jesus gives us His strength, and we're able to do what appears to be impossible—just like Peter.

What glorious liberty exists when we apply the principle of submission to our lives! Defenses come tumbling down. We stand totally open before the Lord and others. We abide in constant fellowship with His Spirit.

Through submission, we can know what it means to be truly liberated. We can be filled with faith, free at last to become everything God created us to be!

Other Books by
P.B. Wilson

⤳

Betrayal's Baby
Turning the Bitter to Sweet

God Is in the Bedroom Too
The Pleasures of True Intimacy

God Is in the Kitchen Too
*Experiencing Blessing Where You Thought
You'd Never Find It*

Majoring in Your Marriage
12 Ways to Improve Your Relationship

Night Come Swiftly
(A novel)

Seven Secrets Women Want to Know

Your Knight in Shining Armor
Discovering Your Lifelong Love

⤳

These books may be obtained at your
local Christian bookstore or at
www.frankandbunny.com